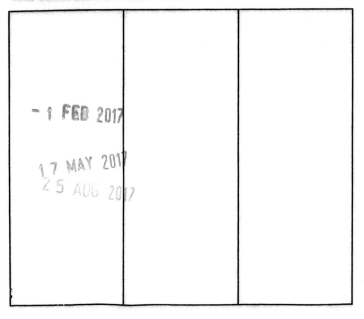

WE ARE THE
56

THE INDIVIDUALS BEHIND A POLITICAL REVOLUTION

WE ARE THE

56

JOSH BIRCHAM AND GRANT COSTELLO

**FREIGHT
BOOKS**

First published 2015

Freight Books
49-53 Virginia Street
Glasgow, G1 1TS
www.freightbooks.co.uk

A CIP catalogue reference for this book is available from the British Library

ISBN 978-1-910449-51-6
eISBN 978-1-910449-52-3

Typeset by Freight in Plantin
Printed and bound by Hussar Books, Poland

the publisher acknowledges investment from
Creative Scotland toward the publication of this book

For Rosie, for all your help and patience.

For Mum and Grandpa, without you I could never have done this.
Wish you'd been here to see it all happen.

PREFACE

This book was conceived on the morning of the 8th May 2015, following the election for the 56th Westminster Parliament, when the political map of Scotland changed, arguably more dramatically than it had done since the Act of Union in 1707.

Due to the vagaries of the first-past-the-post system, with 50% of the overall vote, the Scottish National Party won 56 of the 59 seats being contested in Scotland, gathering 1,454,436 votes, tripling its vote since the last election in 2010. Scottish Labour, who had dominated Westminster politics north of the border for decades, lost all but one of its 41 seats.

Regardless of one's political affiliation, this was an astounding result and not one that the media or pollsters had predicted. Post-referendum, with the disappointment of a No vote still raw for supporters of Independence, many of those standing as prospective parliamentary candidates for the SNP in traditionally safe Labour seats had not realistically expected to get elected. Having followed the campaign closely, I reckoned that 20 or 25 seats would be an outstanding result for the SNP, considering they had held a whopping 6 seats in Westminster since 2010.

As I sat on the sofa on the 8th May, sipping from my cup of tea, watching the results and analysis on breakfast TV, I tried to understand what had just happened. But one thought dominated. Who were these people who had been in the vanguard of a peaceful but dramatic political revolution?

For me, one of the most noticeable differences between the SNP and Scottish Labour during the election campaign had been the proportion of 'ordinary folk' who had been selected to contest seats, people energised and engaged as a result of the Referendum and with little or no direct experience of frontline politics. There were of course still a number of long-standing activists and apparatchiks from within the SNP ranks, but I was particularly interested to find out exactly who would be representing Scotland in the UK parliament. Just as with the Referendum, and the huge ground-swell of political engagement that occurred in Scotland, politicians seemed far closer to ordinary voters like me than they had ever been.

So I decided to commission a book of interviews with all 56 SNP MPs in order to hear from them, in their own words, what motivated them to stand, what values they have taken to Westminster, and what their impression is of the UK political system. As much as anything, that was a book that I wanted to read myself.

I was lucky to know of two young men, politically engaged and with experience in journalism, who had recently completed their studies at the University of Aberdeen. One was my nephew, Josh Bircham, and the other his best friend, Grant Costello. Together they had co-edited the *Goudie*, the Aberdeen University student newspaper.

Within a day or two Josh and Grant were signed up and we were planning the best way to make this book happen. It is testament to their energy and determination that, as the 56 took their seats, found constituency and parliamentary offices and staff, and tried to get their heads around the arcane protocol of the Palace of Westminster – with many, many other things to think about as well – that Josh and Grant managed to secure valuable time in the exceptionally busy diaries of each.

It is my hope that this book gives readers a picture of why ordinary Scots choose to enter politics, what their hopes and dreams are, what kind of backgrounds have shaped their political views and what the early days of the new parliament have been like. Intentionally, this isn't a book of political analysis, written by the cadre of commentators that dominate Scotland, but an introduction to each of the 56 MPs individually.

Most importantly, I hope *We are the 56* reinforces the message that each and every one of these Members of Parliament are here to represent us, their constituents, a privilege and huge responsibility.

Adrian Searle
Freight Books

INTRODUCTION

The May 2015 general election wasn't just any old election. It was a defining moment in Scottish history. Never before had Scottish voters united on this scale across class, religious and regional divisions in support of one political party: the Scottish National Party.

The SNP went from 6 seats out of 59 in 2010 to 56 seats out of 59 five years later. In general elections swings rarely reach double figures. In May 2015, the average swing was 30%, and in Glasgow North, supposedly one of Labour's safest seats, it reached 39%, breaking the BBC's swingometer. Results like these are simply unprecedented in Scottish or UK politics.

The SNP had never won a seat in Glasgow before – a Labour citadel for a century; now they hold all seven of them. The Liberal Democrats who had dominated much of the north of Scotland and parts of the Borders, were wiped off the Scottish mainland.

From the housing estates of West Central Scotland to the landed estates of Perthshire; from oil-rich Aberdeen in the North East to the scattered islands off the West coast; from the borders to the highlands, the SNP drove all before it. It was an extraordinary political event, a tsunami, almost a peaceful revolution.

It was all the more remarkable for the fact that this tsunami struck only nine months after Scottish voters had rejected independence in the referendum of September 2014. Clearly, the referendum had not resolved the constitutional question. The party of independence experienced a membership explosion as tens of thousands joined up and made the SNP the third largest party in the UK with 110,000 members.

Nicola Sturgeon must take much of the credit for leading this surge of support so adroitly and translating it into victory at the ballot box in 2015. Her performance in the leadership debates during the general election campaign won widespread plaudits – and not just from Scottish voters. Indeed, according to some polls she was the most persuasive leader in the entire UK.

But leaders don't win elections on their own. It takes huge organisation and dedicated candidates on the ground, pounding the streets, knocking on doors, stuffing envelopes and speaking in hustings events. This election may have been a landslide, but every vote had to be won by argument and persistence against a background of a media which is generally hostile to Scottish nationalism.

Candidates like Tommy Sheppard, the new MP for Edinburgh East, one of the safest Labour seats in Scotland which had been in the party's hands since 1924. Sheppard is in many ways typical of the 56 in that he defies the media's stereotype of an SNP MP. He is a former assistant secretary of the Labour Party, a businessman who built The Stand chain of comedy venues and calls himself an internationalist.

On the other side of Scotland, another extraordinary contest took place in Paisley and Renfrewshire South between one of Labour's most senior former cabinet ministers, Douglas Alexander, and a 20 year old politics student and charity worker, Mhairi Black. Against all the odds she won by arguing the case for independence doorstep to doorstep, street by street.

These are names already familiar to most – indeed, Mhairi Black became an internet sensation when her maiden speech in the House of Commons was viewed over 10 million times. But most of the 56 MPs on the opposition benches are less well known. This book is an opportunity for them to introduce themselves – as much as possible in their own words – and explain where they came from and how they see the future of the 56 and of Scotland.

Iain Macwhirter

1. ALEX SALMOND
GORDON

'The 56 are fantastic,' said Alex Salmond 'I loved the group in the Scottish Parliament between 2007 and 2011 because they were so loyal under the most extraordinary circumstances and they would go through fire to maintain the government. In terms of talent, raw political talent, and breadth of ability, this is an extraordinary group and a deep reservoir of skilled politicians.' This is high praise indeed from the man who steered the SNP from obscurity into the national party of Scotland.

As such a high profile figure, Alex's early life has been well documented. He grew up in Linlithgow and had 'an incredibly well grounded childhood'. He describes his upbringing as privileged; not in the traditional sense of the word, but in the fact he had loving parents, supportive siblings, grandparents close by, and a great deal of advice and encouragement. He reminisces about his schooling: 'I always remember there was a television programme (when the BBC still made television programmes) about twenty years ago that followed the life of a community school in Scotland. It was one of these fly-on-the-wall documentaries, and they asked the rector then how he would describe his school and he said 'just a typical Scottish small town comprehensive,' before turning around and looking into the camera and saying, 'of which no praise could be higher.' Well, I went to a small school and had a small town Scottish upbringing in a council scheme with a strong, distinct, and loyal community, of which no praise could be higher.'

Like his three siblings Alex went to university 'which was tough even in the days with no fees and a maximum grant'. His parents were the 'driving force' behind his education and were convinced that their children should have the best chance in life. Alex was always the rebel and he remembers when he was fifteen when his friends were all leaving to get jobs. He saw the idea of earning money as an attractive prospect: 'I went over to the brickworks in Whitecross for a holiday job and I got my uncle Andy to get me a job because he was a foreman. I initially got the job for the holiday but I planned to extend it. I announced this to my mother and she didn't say anything at all which was strange because I was expecting strong opposition to this ridiculous idea. When I started working there I found myself doing the dirtiest, most strenuous, backbreaking, mind-numbing, and dangerous jobs you could imagine. I was shifting amphasite, which is something you really don't want to do. This was the days before health and safety and there were no face masks or anything, and I was asthmatic.'

'While working at the brickworks it was one of only two times in my life that I've sleepwalked. The other time was when I was expelled from the SNP a number of years after that. There was a disturbance that things that were not quite right manifested by sleepwalking. After a few weeks of this backbreaking miserable existence – which seemed well remunerated at the time but, if I remember right, I got £11, £14 with overtime a week – I announced to my mother that I would be going back to school after all. She said nothing, just a 'that's fine'. This was in about 1970, and in 1977 my uncle Andrew was running me though to St Andrews University because he had a car. He was retired by then and he said to me, "I've always been a bit guilty about something, Alec. You remember a few years ago when you worked for the brickworks and I was the foreman and you ended up with the worst jobs in the entire plant? That was your mum. She telt me that if you stayed in the brickwork then I wouldny be welcome in your hoose any more and therefore I had no choice in the matter." I found that my mum had conspired against me, out of love obviously! Once you've done six or seven weeks shifting amphasite then the idea of becoming an economist has a new lustre.'

After school Alex initially considered going into the advertising industry or business journalism. After spending some time at the College of Commerce after his sixth year at school, he realised that this wasn't something that he wanted to do after all. He had, however, studied a course at college in Economics which he had found 'really interesting'. When Alex started he studied Medieval and Modern History but fell out with the Modern History department quite badly due to a right-wing lecturer called Norman Gash, (or as Alex called him, 'Gash the Fash'). His abandonment of Modern History could also have been because he didn't turn up to any classes. When he left Modern History he combined Mediaeval History with a side course in Economics he had taken because he 'knew how to do it as he had done it before'. Alex explained: 'The mediaeval history department was just my metre. They loved my unorthodox view of the world. I also got to study under Geoffrey Barrow. He was an extraordinary narrative historian and I was one of only four people in his honours year. Then, of course, to study Scottish history itself was a challenge at St Andrews. To be allowed in, you had to turn up at the old quad, knock three times, and ask for Geoffrey. I was the first person to ever do the joint honours of Economics and Mediaeval History in about twenty-five years. Joint honours, of course, is the thing you should absolutely do as the Mediaeval department believed I was in Economics, and the Economics department believed I was in Mediaeval History when, in actual fact, I was out campaigning for the SNP in some godforsaken by-election.'

Alex entered the Government Economic Service as an Assistant Economist in the Department of Agriculture and Fisheries for Scotland almost immediately after leaving university. He then joined the staff of the Royal Bank of Scotland two years later, where he worked for seven years, initially as an Assistant Economist. In 1982 he became an Oil Economist, and from 1984 a Bank Economist, while continuing to hold the position of Oil Economist. Alex's study of Economics has been a consistent and visible part of his professional and then-political life, but his study of Mediaeval History also made an impact on many of his views: 'As an English poet once said, "Full many a flower is born to blush unseen, and waste his sweetness in the desert air" – the mediaeval world was many flowers blushing unseen, unable to be sophisticated because of the lack of information and learning available. It was, of course, Scotland that had the genius to take the country out of the mediaeval world into the modern world by introducing universal education, meaning fewer flowers of Scotland blush unseen.'

Alex was not always a member of the SNP, describing himself as originally 'favourable to Labour'. However, his dad was a strong SNP supporter and the younger man would always side with him when things got heated in political arguments; his parents 'hardly talked about politics but when they did it was pretty ferocious'. Alex also remembers when he stood as the SNP candidate in a school election: 'mind you that was the last party available, but I did win the election'.

Alex had a strong grounding in the SNP through growing up knowing the potential of Scotland and the Scottish people: 'My whole background and upbringing told me that ordinary people could do extraordinary things [...] I remember once when I was on holiday in Colonsay and I was talking to [...] a crab and lobster fisherman with just a wee boat. He was talking about the department of agriculture and fisheries like he knew them, personally mentioning Jeremy from the department and the fact he told him that they should do this and that; he thought he was on an equal par with them which is a great view of the world to have. I think the view of the world I was given in Linlithgow was something like that – you can achieve anything if you put your mind to it. I also had a Presbyterian upbringing which supported and reinforced that.'

Many of the 56 have talked about the changing perspectives towards the SNP and indeed independence, which led to the momentous 2015 General Election result. Alex talked about the shift in people's thinking during the Referendum, when people retaliated against the constant 'you can't' message of the unionist campaign. Members of the 56 such as Angus MacNeil and Joanna Cherry have made reference to the enormous sacrifice that Alex made stepping down as the First Minister, despite still having the support of the party and 45% of the population. Alex explained why he had to step down: 'When I heard Cameron's speech I knew there was a huge political opportunity for the SNP. I also knew it was important that someone took responsibility because we had lost and you've got to clear the decks with these things and take advantage of that opportunity. I've always been very instinctive with these things. I feel like I know this country and its people very well, and I feel like I know what's important. It was a hell of a speech though, a hell of a speech.'

Many of the 56 have cited Alex as their inspiration. Alex responded to this: 'It's very humbling to be called an inspiration as these are talented folk. [...] My political hero is Mandela which is conventional to people of my generation but he's a man that's changed more perspectives than anyone else.' Changing perspectives is what Alex and the 56 generally hope to achieve. Alex discussed using inspiration to change the 'colour of people's thought' before explaining the origins of that quote: 'the phrase "the colour of thought" is taken from R. S. Thomas, a Welsh poet, in a poem about an ancient Welsh hero called Garaldis, who changed the colour of his thought about Wales when he drank from the Welsh fountain. I hope that through [the Referendum and the General Election] the colour of people's thought has been changed and changed for the better.'

Like every one of the SNP MPs, Alex has a vision for Scotland: 'I think that this could be a really special country. No country is perfect and there will be a lot of challenges and things to overcome but I think we have the ingredients to make this a great country. We have a huge reservoir bequeathed to us in terms of the people, the land, the tradition, and the reputation, which are enormous assets, and we could make something really special of this country.' Alex then paused before looking over and saying with genuine emotion: 'I think most people are proud of being Scottish. There are a few exceptions I have met, but most people are. It would be great if we could live up to that self-estimation, not just as individuals, but collectively.'

2. CHRIS LAW
DUNDEE WEST

In the 2015 General Election Chris Law won the seat of Dundee West with the largest majority of the SNP – 61.9% – taking the seat from Labour who had held it for the past sixty-five years. Chris was born in Edinburgh and grew up in Fife until his mid-teens. He attended Glenwood High in Glenrothes then later Madras College in St Andrews. Describing school as a 'period of containment', Chris left school before his sixteenth birthday and went to college to train as a chef in French and Scottish cuisine.

Chris worked full-time as a chef until he was about nineteen then, at twenty, he went back to college because he wanted to go to university. He studied Modern Studies, A-level Politics and A-level Sociology. Talking about this time Chris revealed: 'I had a fantastic teacher, which totally inspired my journey into politics and social sciences.' After leaving college Chris lived in Europe for a year and then India for another year. After his time abroad Chris went to university: 'When I came back my original plan was do either Law or Psychology. In the end I decided to do Social Anthropology which is more in tune with what I was enjoying at the time, and I studied at St Andrews in the 90s in my mid-twenties. I did my degree in Social Anthropology and my postgraduate [degree] in IT.'

'Whilst I was at university I set up my first business – I always had an entrepreneurial streak – going on expeditions through the Himalayas, on 1950s motorbikes in North India up to the world's highest road. I never earned a penny doing it but I learnt a lot about business skills and all the rest. Then post-university I thought I fancied getting a graduate job at a management consultancy firm, but then very quickly realised that it wasn't for me! I then worked in social documentary filmmaking for a few years and I spent a spell with Raleigh International in Namibia. Then I worked in financial services over the last ten years. All of that time I had my own companies, though the only one I've ever made a living off is my last one! During that time I was always politically interested in what was going on. I think when the crash in 2009 hit, the industry I was in had 90% of my fellow colleges losing their jobs, not in my business but in other businesses. I started to ask questions about the UK economy. I rejoined the SNP at that point; I had been a member while I was student which I had let lapse. I rejoined and got involved at branch level once the Referendum had been announced.'

Chris was a prominent figure during the Scottish Referendum, founding The Spirit of Independence organisation that campaigned around Scotland in a 1950s Green Goddess fire engine. Chris spoke about his experience of the Referendum campaign: 'I was involved from the very beginning. I really felt that what was good about the entire Referendum period was that it was above and beyond party politics. It was a great emotional, mental, and physical space to be in to explore ideas about what sort of society you wanted to be in. If you could find that space then you could really explore, investigate, and scrutinise what you were trying to achieve.'

'In early 2014 I was out knocking on doors with Radical Independence and I was involved with the SNP at branch level and also Business for Scotland, because I had a small business. What I recognised were two key things: there was a lack of information as well as an inherent London-centric bias of the media. I wanted to challenge that head-on. I wanted to create something inspirational that was visual and something that would capture the media's imagination as well as people's imagination, which is why I set up the Spirit of Independence organisation.'

'We needed something very visual that carried as many different organisations' material as possible. A 1950s Green Goddess fire engine might not be the first thing that springs to mind, but it was really the best tool for the job! It was very striking. I've got lots of great stories of how [the organisation] engaged people, but one in particular [...] happened in Kirkcudbright down in Dumfries where there was no visible Yes group and no conversation going on in the local school. It was considered to be a strong unionist/Tory area. We were invited down [...] in the morning and went down to the harbour and did an interview with Richard Lochhead and another MSP, and in the school there was a bit of a mini-revolution. There had been utterly no conversation and in the morning break teachers went back to their staffroom and one teacher asked another whether they'd seen the vehicle outside. The answer was 'yes' and they asked 'What are your thoughts on independence?' and they said 'Oh, well I'll be voting yes.' 'Really?' and other people went 'Oh, I will be as well!', and this all sparked conversations which spread out into the classrooms later. At lunchtime I saw four teachers coming down with about thirty or forty kids in white shirts and ties to get information. It's interesting because days or weeks after, I was getting feedback from campaigners saying that they could now talk openly about the Referendum so it was excellent as a conversation piece.'

Chris's journey to Westminster after the Referendum was reluctant: 'I had no plans to be an MP – I was actually asking myself prior to the 18th what I would do if it was a No vote. I did think I might leave the country and go travelling for a year or two. What happened for me after the 19th was that I was pretty numb for a couple of days. I got hundreds and hundreds of emails and messages from people from all over the world who had been following what I had been doing, but mainly from Scotland. I also got a huge outpouring of grief from men and women, but particularly from men, in a way I had never received before. Over the next few weeks I found myself replying to these messages. It's quite hard when you read a message from one man, for example, saying he was writing to me with teardrops falling on the keyboard. After three weeks I got the most almighty flu – I think my body had just given up

– and I burst into tears for about an hour. I went forward for vetting and went towards hustings in January, but I would be lying if I said I had the same excitement and positive hopefulness that I did before, as for me now it was a case of wanting to finish what I had started. What I'm learning to be now is a good constituent MP and to represent everybody's interests, no matter what their political views are. It's a real privilege when you learn about people's lives and challenges in doing the job. There's far more to it than simply campaigning for another referendum.'

Chris's inspiration as an MP comes from his mother: 'My mother had severe multiple sclerosis which means she was wheelchair-bound and with all the various sub-conditions that come with it, from inflammation, constant pain, immobility, to the crankiness that comes from it as well, and we argued tooth and nail growing up. Looking back now, I really value that because it taught me to articulate and think about the other point of view. I don't think I made her life easy as a result, but what I value from her is the ability to keep going when everyone else has stopped and that tenacity of character which would keep pressing on, even though you feel like giving up yesterday. I mean, politically it's very easy for me, as I've spent the best part of twenty years coming and going from India so I've read a lot about the independence movement in India, which Ghandi was a big part of. I also worked and lived in Namibia, which is next to South Africa, and Mandela has been a huge influence. Not only have I read most of his stuff but I am one of the worldwide collectors of his memorabilia and bits and pieces which I've done for about twenty years.'

Chris is proud of the fact that Scotland is moving on from a tartan-clad past to a future that has a clear and positive identity. Looking forward he wants to see a Scotland of even greater care and social responsibility: 'This goes back to Leslie Riddoch's book *Blossom* where she describes how part of the culture of looking out for each other goes back to the days when the vast majority of Scots lived in tenements where you knew your close neighbours. I think we can continue developing that sense of common weal and knowing that the balance of a good society is opportunity, productivity, and entrepreneurialism, but it should never be at the expense of those less fortunate.'

3. STEWART HOSIE
DUNDEE EAST

Stewart Hosie described the 2015 General Election as a 'sea change' after he was elected as MP for Dundee East with 28,765 votes – more votes than all of the other candidates put together. Indeed, this landslide victory and 56 Scottish SNP MPs in Westminster would have been almost unthinkable when Stewart joined the party.

Stewart was born in Dundee and attended Brackens Primary School, Invertay Primary School, then Monifieth and Carnoustie High School. He then went on to the Dundee Institute of Technology (now Abertay University) where he gained a Higher Diploma in Computer Studies. After studying at university Stewart went into IT, running his own business in that area.

Stewart talked about where the party was when he joined it aged twenty-two: 'In those days we had two MPs, one MEP, and a handful of councillors. We've come a very long way over the past twenty or thirty years.' Stewart went on to become the SNP's first Youth Convener from 1986 to 1989, in a period dominated by Thatcherite politics. Within his time he saw a resurgence in the party following the 1979 decimation of the SNP.

Stewart's first election campaign was in 1992 for the seat of

Kirkcaldy. He then contested Kirkcaldy again at the 1997 General Election, and then again at the Scottish Parliament General Election in 1999. In 1999 he was elected as the SNP's Organisation Convener. In an interview with *The National* on the 8th June, 2015,Stewart talked about his campaigns prior to running in Dundee East: 'I took a view early on that there was no point waiting for other people to do things, you kind of had to step up yourself. I contested any number of elections in the bad old days. One of the tasks was to eventually stand and win in Dundee East – which we did!'

At the 2001 General Election Stewart contested Dundee East, and reduced the incumbent Labour majority. He then stood again and was elected on the 5th May 2005, taking the seat from Labour. Hosie held the seat with an increased majority at the 2010 General Election before his crushing victory in 2015. 'What that proved – and this is important – was the SNP could beat Labour in what were traditionally heartland seats in a general election'.

After his election to the House of Commons for Dundee East in 2005, Stewart was appointed the SNP spokesperson for Home Affairs and Women, positions that he held until 2007. He was also appointed SNP spokesperson for the Treasury. Then, in 2010, he was appointed Deputy Leader and Chief Whip of the SNP. Since the landslide 2015 Election, Stewart is now the Deputy Group Leader in Westminster under Angus Robertson and also holds the Economy portfolio.

Stewart was involved in the vibrant and very successful Referendum campaign in Dundee, the Yes City, attending and guest speaking at several events, as well as giving the case for a Yes vote at Abertay, his former university. He was very pleased with the local result: 'In Dundee we polled a 57% Yes result but of course nobody can deny that the result was disappointing as across the country we didn't quite do enough.' Following the result, Hosie looked straight to Westminster: 'The 2015 General Election is the Scottish people's chance to hold Westminster's feet to the fire and make them deliver on the devolution they promised.'

At the SNP Conference in November 2014, Stewart was elected Deputy Leader of the SNP, succeeding Nicola Sturgeon, and proudly stood in his position with Nicola at the launch of the SNP's Westminster manifesto. Stewart's personal 2015 Election campaign was fired by the energy of the independence Referendum. He explained that 'the people who joined the SNP did not join the party to change it, they joined it to be part of it and carry on the campaign for Scottish independence. The main influence to the campaign is the new membership; they've come from the activism of the Yes campaign and you can see the impact of that.'

Since becoming an MP, Stewart has widely criticised the Welfare Reform Act 2012, as well as the Prudential Regulation Authority. In Westminster he plans to focus on the Tories' austerity measures, including the welfare cuts; his position on the Commons Treasury Select Committee gives him added insight: 'We've got a mandate to bring to the Commons genuine opposition to the UK Government, in particular a genuinely different approach to the economy,' he said. 'When we say 'a real end to austerity', we mean it.' He also highlighted the impacts of these policies in Scotland: 'Westminster's obsession with austerity is holding back Scotland's economy and damaging communities across the country, pushing 100,000 more children in Scotland into poverty and seeing a 400% increase in people forced to rely on foodbanks.'

Stewart has also condemned Labour's lack of action on the Tories' economic policies – they have 'shamefully backed George Osborne's plans' – while 'both [the Conservatives and Labour] are wedded to the same austerity agenda while supporting spending £100bn on a new generation of weapons of mass destruction. This isn't just economically illiterate – it is morally indefensible.'

Speaking of the new SNP group, Stewart echoed the sentiment of other MPs who had previously sat in Westminster: 'What I'm finding is that the quality is incredibly high. It only took a few days at Westminster and the Maiden Speeches to start for some of the rather snide comments about the quality of our new members to be completely put to bed.'

4. STUART DONALDSON
WEST ABERDEENSHIRE AND KINCARDINE

'For a long time the SNP was synonymous with things I didn't want to do. I would have rather hung out with my friends than go to SNP meetings, of which there always seemed to be an awful lot,' joked the SNP's second youngest MP. Growing up in Aberdeenshire, the SNP was just part of daily life for Stuart Donaldson's family. His grandfather was the SNP MP for Banffshire, winning the seat and holding it during the twin elections of 1974, and was later an SNP Councillor. The political bug was then passed on to Stuart's mother, Maureen Watt, who was elected to the Scottish Parliament in 2006. Both his mother and grandfather stood for election multiple times, so Stuart found himself the young gun in photos, out supporting his political family. As with most children, doing what your parents want is not exactly the style, and Stuart felt the need to rebel against the SNP.

Stuart did not want a career in politics and instead wanted to be a stuntman. Fast cars, loud noises, and being on a movie set was his vision of the future while at Banchory Academy, definitely not parliament or the SNP. He tried to ignore politics altogether, even refusing to take Modern Studies at high school until crashing the subject in his final year: 'When I was starting to think about university […] I realised I knew a lot about Modern Studies, so I crashed it and got an A.' This was the first crack in his ardent opposition to politics: having enjoyed Modern Studies he choose to study Politics at the University of Glasgow.

At university his early opposition to politics manifested itself as an opposition to party politics. 'I wanted to approach politics from an academic background rather than a partisan background,' he said. As he got more and more interested in politics and developed an outlook on the political scene, he began to realise that the views and opinions he held were those espoused by the SNP and his mum, now a government Minister. By his third year at university his rebellion against the SNP had been replaced with admiration, especially for the SNP's Humza Yousaf. It was the young MSP's ability to 'speak the politics of fluent human' which had so impressed Stuart. This admiration didn't stop just with Yousaf but spread across the whole SNP administration. Stuart finally began to feel at home within the SNP.

After the election of the SNP in 2011, Stuart started to be much more involved, taking up a key role within the local Yes Aberdeenshire group and coordinating local activities. Later, he joined Christian Allard, the recently elected MSP for the North East Regional List in 2013, as a Parliamentary Officer. Even though he had now become a fully fledged member of the SNP it wasn't about starting a career in politics for Stuart. In fact, he had planned to move to China and start a career in tourism. Having studied Mandarin at night classes in his final year at university, Stuart saw the opportunity to go to China and do something different. He didn't want the life of a politician, and working on the Yes campaign centred on his passion to see an independent Scotland. After it was over he wanted to see the world: 'I started to get things lined up to go to China, but when we lost the Referendum people started asking me to stand.'

Stuart's decision to stand wasn't taken lightly, and months passed before he decided. He had conversations with his mum and girlfriend who regularly urged him to stand, and his boss Christian Allard also strongly supported the idea of him putting his hat in the ring. In the end it was the despair at the Referendum result that really started to turn his mind to the possibility of standing for election. 'It wasn't about going to Westminster,' he said. 'It was really about representing the place I grew up in and had lived my whole life. I wouldn't be in politics if I couldn't have run for my constituency. It was very much about this election and my constituency.' The pull of standing for the place in which he had grown up was too much to turn down and Stuart later admits that if he hadn't stood 'I would have regretted what might have been.'

Stuart had a belief that, despite very strong local campaigns from the Conservatives and Liberal Democrats hoping to win the seat, the campaign from the local activist base would push him forward. The Conservatives and Liberal Democrats had student activists regularly coming from the University of Aberdeen and Robert Gordon University to campaign, but Stuart tried to keep his campaign local and positive with a big boost from the Lord Ashcroft Poll: '[the] Ashcroft Poll gave everyone a moral boost. But did we sit back and say 'we can relax now'? No – the poll very much spurred us on.'

On election night he remained stone-faced throughout the whole count, even when ballot box sampling seemed to suggest that it was going to be a victory. Having been through the Referendum, Stuart feared that it could all end up being another terrible defeat: 'People were coming up to congratulate me, but I was still waiting until I heard the results'. Stuart took the seat on a 21.5% swing from the Liberal Democrats, in the same hall that, only months prior, had delivered the heart-wrenching results of the Referendum. 'When the result came in it was just unreal: the same faces that months ago had been absolutley devastated were now so delighted at what we had achieved.'

The political revolution of the SNP is nowhere more evident than in the constituency of West Aberdeenshire and Kincardine, where both the constituency and Stuart transformed over time to find themselves at home with the SNP as a political party. For Stuart, though, it is now all about standing up for his constituents and Scotland: 'The people and the communities have made me the person that I am today, so it is really now about helping them, but also about standing up and representing Scotland more widely. We try and fulfill the expectations and the trust that the people of Scotland placed on us, and I remember that every single day.'

5. MIKE WEIR
ANGUS

Mike Weir is a veteran of the SNP in Westminster and the party. The 2015 Election saw him elected with 54% of the vote for the Angus constituency, which he has held since 2001. Mike was born in Arbroath in 1958, and he was the first in his family to go to university, studying law at the University of Aberdeen and graduating in 1979. Mike is very grateful for his chance to go to university: 'I was only able to go because in my day there were no tuition fees and you got a student grant and were able to get on with it.' Whilst at university Mike served as President of the Aberdeen University Scottish Nationalist Association, and was also a member of the Student Representative Council. He also joined the SNP.

Mike has always been a nationalist and believed in independence. He remembers the first time he became interested was in 1974 when there were two general elections. It was also a year of significant success for SNP MPs, rising from one to seven; Mike was in high school during this election and he remembers handing out leaflets for the party.

After leaving university Mike went into law, working as a solicitor around Montrose and Kirkcaldy country before settling in Brechin and becoming a partner in the firm J&DG Shiell. Mike's political career started in 1984 when he served as a councillor on Angus District Council, where he held the position of Convenor of General Purposes. Then in 1987, Mike stood as the SNP candidate in Aberdeen South.

By the time he was elected as one of the 56 in 2015, Mike was entering his fourteenth year as an MP. While at Westminster he has served in numerous positions including SNP Spokesperson on Trade and Industry and Work and Pensions, SNP Westminster Spokesperson on Business and Enterprise (which includes Energy and the Environment), as well as sitting on several committees. When asked about what his main concerns are in this parliament Mike replied: 'I am a firm believer in Scottish independence and I may well want to push that forward, but I also believe in social justice and equality. I feel that we will have to fight hard in this parliament against the Tory Government, especially with what they want to do in these areas. You just have to look at what's happened in their welfare reform bill and their budget. The less well off in our society will find this all much harder than the rich. We really need to fight that and produce a more equal society.'

Mike still hasn't got used to some aspects of the House of Commons, despite his lengthy experience of Westminster: 'It's like working in Hogwarts really, it's a throw-back to god knows when. It really needs to modernise. When you look at Westminster compared to the Scottish Parliament it's obvious. One simple thing is we have to queue up and have our names ticked off a register when we vote – in the age of electronics it's completely ludicrous and time-consuming. All the ceremony is dated and we need to bring the parliament into the twenty-first century.'

Mike will spend a lot of his time in the chamber this parliament due to his position as the SNP's Chief Whip. Yet it hasn't been difficult to get the 56 into the chamber so far as they 'are a determined group with a mission where everyone is buckling down and getting to work.' Mike explained that he is always learning: 'I mean, it's all new to me, I've never been a whip before and Chief Whip is new to me. We're all learning together as we go along. We've gone from being a group of 6 to a group of 56 so it's been a very steep learning curve for everyone involved.'

When asked about how he found 2014's Referendum campaign Mike answered: 'Well, it was exhausting. I think my experience [...] was all very positive, apart from the result obviously. As the campaign went on it became obvious that we had a far greater level of engagement with people than we have had before, and the campaign was positive in that sense. It was really refreshing to knock on someone's door and have them [be] really keen to speak to you about independence, which is the reverse to what normally used to happen prior to that in political campaigns, where you had to drag them to the door and drag them into speaking to you. People wanted to speak about it. I always remember knocking on people's doors to have them say they were just discussing the issues on Saturday night, or in work or in the pub and 'what about these things?' It was a real change and a really exhilarating experience when people were truly engaged, whatever their views, wanting to discuss it and discuss their options. In the end we didn't win, but we got 45% to vote for independence which I think is a tremendous move forward. I think what has happened since has just shown how a more engaged society changes politics.'

Mike is married with two daughters and also enjoys spending as much time with them as possible when he has time away from Westminster. He talked about what he would like to see for Scotland: 'I want Scotland to be a fairer society that looks after everybody in it, one where everybody gets every opportunity they can, whatever their background. For example I had the opportunity to go to university because of my fees being paid and a grant. I've also been very grateful to the National Health Service in the course of my life. These are things that are frightfully important to me and are things that should be the bedrock of any society – to make sure that education, health and housing are available to everybody.'

6. KIRSTY BLACKMAN
ABERDEEN NORTH

Kirsty Ann Blackman, born in Aberdeen in 1986, was raised in a small village on the Banffshire coast until she was five years old, when her family moved back into the city centre of Aberdeen. Growing up, Kirsty was close to all her siblings – her brother John is three years younger and her two sisters ten years younger – and Kirsty would often take it as her duty to look after them on family holidays: 'We were not a family that just sat down and watched TV. We were always out and about, going away at weekends, out in the caravan or visiting historical places.'

Kirsty couldn't stay the big sister forever, though. Smart at high school with good grades, she decided that university beckoned. Although it meant leaving her siblings behind, she wanted to become a doctor. However, being a medical student wasn't exactly what she had hoped for: 'I wanted to help people and I thought I could do that by being a doctor, and you can do that by being a doctor, but you can't do that by being a medical student. I just thought I cannot cope with five years of learning how cells talk to each other because I'm going to go insane.' During Kirsty's first year at the University of Aberdeen she realised that she had never actually wanted to become a doctor.

Convinced that she couldn't undertake another four years of theoretical medicine, she decided to drop out of the medical degree. She joked that 'I still think that the job would be quite good, but I'm just not willing to do the training.'

Still determined to help people, she found a job as a care assistant in a nursing home. Originally Kirsty thought that the job would be the ideal halfway point between her wish to help people and her earlier ambition to become a doctor: as a care assistant she hoped she would be able to help to ensure that everyone received the care and attention they required. Yet this role just didn't feel right, and Kirsty explained how she felt she couldn't support people in the way she wanted: 'I didn't think that people were getting a good quality of life, so... I decided it wasn't for me.'

Leaving in early 2006, Kirsty applied for a temping agency hoping that she would be able to find work quickly. Her ability to touch type meant that she was quickly hired by a local agency and sent to work within Aberdeen Council's planning department. Despite her initial reservations, this job was in fact extremely enjoyable, and Kirsty was soon offered a permanent post. This was, however, short-lived because Kirsty was offered the position of Caseworker for the SNP MSP Brian Adam. Having joined the SNP when she was fourteen and serving as secretary of her local SNP branch, Kirsty was well known to many SNP activists and had heavily campaigned for Adam's election in 2003. Despite the fact that she really enjoyed working for the council, she could not turn down the opportunity to work for Brian Adam: 'I felt quite bad leaving the council [...] but this was much more aligned with what I wanted to do right then.'

Working for Brian Adam also presented Kirsty with time to get much more involved with the SNP. Kevin Stewart, the SNP's leader on Aberdeen Council and future MSP, convinced her to stand for council elections: 'I didn't need much arm twisting [from Kevin Stewart] because I didn't know where I was going and thought this is something I could do to help people so I went for it.' At the same time, she was also asked to become the election agent for Aberdeen Central's SNP candidate Karen Shirron. This seat was considered to be a possible gain for the SNP, and Kirsty embraced the opportunity, hoping to play her part in acquiring other SNP MSPs for the city. On election night in 2007 the SNP failed to capture Aberdeen Central by 349 votes, and as the election agent, Kirsty had to ask for a recount which she later described as 'one of the most nerve-racking experiences of my life yet'. The recount only confirmed that the SNP hadn't picked up the seat, but the party would make major gains in the council elections by becoming part of an SNP-Liberal Democrat administration.

While Kirsty had expected to win her seat on the council it was a shock that her younger brother John, only eighteen, had also been elected. Soon afterwards they both found themselves with positions in the city's new administration: 'I became the Education Spokesperson and John [became] Depute Provost, it was incredible.' This new SNP group would become well known throughout Scotland for its many elected young faces, including the future MP Callum McCaig and the future MSP Mark McDonald.

Over the next five years Kirsty served in multiple positions while fielding many questions about whether she saw herself running for either parliament in the near future: 'People asked me if the council was a stepping stone and I have always said no, and always meant it. [Running for parliament] was never something that was in my game plan.' Defiant that she would not run for parliament, she even resisted those urging her to run for the Scottish Parliament in 2011. For her it was about the movement of the SNP and independence; following the election of the SNP majority government in 2011, she went on to coordinate the whole of Aberdeen's Yes campaign.

Referendum night, however, brought painful defeat with over 60% of Aberdeen voting No. Kirsty had been chosen to collate the ballot box sampling on the night: 'I remember I left the count early. I felt like I was going to cry, and knew if I cried in the counting hall in Aberdeen I would be on TV, so I left and drove home.' When the results were announced the next morning, Kirsty, her husband, and her two young children, were already on their way to Aviemore. Her plan was to relax in Aviemore and have a weekend away from politics and the Referendum with her family. The only person that knew her whereabouts was Kevin Stewart, but even then, talking to him over the phone reduced her to tears again. However, as the SNP surged in membership and the reaction to the defeat in the Referendum became evident, she knew that she was going to stand for Parliament in 2015: 'I just thought [that] I needed to stand.'

For the next eight months Kirsty went straight back into election mode, and as time went on, it looked like she could really win the seat. However, unlike many of her colleagues, her seat never received a national pollster's in-depth polling, and as election night approached there was a genuine fear that all the canvassing data could be wrong and that Labour would hold the seat. But that all changed, as Kirsty explained: 'I was at my parents' house when the exit poll came out. It corroborated all the results we had been seeing and I was sure we had won it then.' Kirsty, whose Labour opponent was the current regional list MSP Richard Bake, succeeded in overturning an 8361 majority and claiming a 13,396 majority of her own – far bigger than her fellow Aberdeen MP Callum McCaig, which she enjoys reminding people. She would become the first ever SNP MP elected by the City of Aberdeen, following in the footsteps of the now late Brian Adam (who was the first ever constituency MSP elected by the City of Aberdeen).

Reflecting on her victory, she can't but help think of what Brian Adam would have thought of her own and the SNP's success: 'I think he would definitely be proud. He was really good to me. [...] Brian is the reason that those of us round here have an ethos for casework. [...] He always said that the most important thing was casework, it was to do your best for people and try and make life better for people. He was so absolutely right.'

7. CALLUM MCCAIG
ABERDEEN SOUTH

Callum McCaig was born in Edinburgh. The son of two university scientists, his family moved to Aberdeen when he was eighteen months old. The Granite City, a newly affordable destination due to the oil slump in 1986, became his childhood home after both his parents secured jobs in Aberdeen's academic institutions.

It wouldn't be long, however, before Callum trekked back down to the capital to study at the University of Edinburgh: 'I was tempted to study Biology,' he said, 'but both my folks are scientists, so there was probably a bit of a rebellion in not going down the science route.' Instead, he chose to study Politics, as he explained: 'With science there is a right answer and a wrong answer, but with politics there is a debate to be had. That was what attracted politics to me, that by your argument you can change folks' minds.'

Throughout university Callum did not join any of the university political societies: 'It just didn't capture my imagination,' he said. In his final year of university he eventually joined the SNP after his sister had joined and shown him how to do it himself: 'I had always been an SNP supporter, my folks were always supporters, so it just seemed like the natural thing to do was to join the party.' Not long after joining the party officially he attended a lecture at the University of Edinburgh by Alex Salmond. The possibility of the SNP actually winning the Scottish elections was starting to become real and he was excited at the prospect: 'I listened to Alex Salmond speaking about how he was intending to win the election and I thought, I want see what I can do to make that happen.'

After graduating from university, Callum moved back to Aberdeen to live with his parents. He found a job working in the local Sainsbury's, but wanted to find employment that would enable him to get more involved in the SNP and the election campaign. He 'sent Maureen Watt, who was my local MSP, an e-mail asking to come in and volunteer during the campaign. [...] I met with her and spoke for a bit, then a week later she asked if I would be interested in coming to work for her.' It was the right place and the right time for Callum: Maureen Watt had just taken her seat in parliament due to Richard Lochhead's decision to resign in order to fight the Moray by-election, and she didn't have any staff. An enthusiastic graduate like Callum was just what she needed.

Callum seized the opportunity instantly and started working in Maureen Watt's office alongside the SNP's leader in the Aberdeen council Kevin Stewart, who had been helping out part-time. It wasn't long before Kevin Stewart had convinced Callum to put his name forward as a council candidate in the 2007 election; Callum was one of a group of intelligent young SNP supporters that Kevin Stewart convinced to stand for election, and it was the first time that the council elections would be contested under the STV electoral system. It was hoped that many of this group would be elected and become a much larger opposition group in the council. It turned out to be a big night for the SNP at council level with the party doubling its number of seats. For Callum, easily elected on the first ballot and topping the poll in his ward, it was a huge personal triumph.

Over subsequent days it became clear that the SNP was to be part of Aberdeen Council's next administration, and Callum was told that he would be chairing the licensing board. Having been elected and then given a position with the council's administration, Callum was determined to get to work without too much publicity. Thankfully, John West would ensure that wasn't an issue: 'I was just able to get on with things and learn stuff thankfully and John took all the publicity and attention from being named Depute Provost.'

By the 2011 Scottish Elections, Kevin Stewart, who had until then been the SNP Group Leader and Depute Council Leader, succeeded in being elected to the Scottish Parliament as the member for Aberdeen Central. As a result, he resigned from his leadership positions, and Callum was chosen to take over the position of Group Leader and Deputy Council Leader. This new position wouldn't last long as within a month, due to victories in council by-elections, the SNP would become the largest party on the council and Callum was promoted to the position of Council Leader. Aged twenty-six, he became the second youngest council leader in the UK. Later that year the SNP increased its number of councillors at the 2012 council elections, but a Labour-Conservative-Independent coalition formed a majority administration and Callum reverted to the position of Leader of the Opposition on the council.

It was a blow to Callum when the SNP lost Aberdeen Council, but it meant that the next few years could be spent campaigning on the Referendum. As a councillor for Aberdeen South, much of Callum's time was spent campaigning in the suburbs of Aberdeen, trying to convince people that had supported him – and his council administration – that backing independence was also the right thing to do. The 2014 Referendum in Aberdeen would, however, deliver a decisive No vote. Devastated, Callum took time off afterwards to drive down to Edinburgh and escape politics, but enroute he considered the possibility of standing in the General Election. By the time he had reached Edinburgh, however, he decided that he would not stand.

A few days before the close of nominations for the General Election, Callum's father simply asked 'are you sure you're not doing this?'. Despite being adamant that he wouldn't stand, and consistently telling people in his branch this, Callum's father's words made him re-think the situation: 'I began to think that if I could put in a strong challenge in Aberdeen South, Labour would likely focus their efforts there and it would give us the best chance to win Aberdeen North. So I decided to go for it.'

After winning the party's selection, Callum and his election agent

Stephen Flynn decided that it would be best to start campaigning in the areas that the party was weakest. From there they would move into the areas that were strongest, and this approach would ensure that a full campaign was underway in the constituency. Callum's thinking was that, by running a full campaign and really challenging Labour, it would give Kirsty Blackman in Aberdeen North the best chance of winning. As the campaign got underway, areas that Callum thought wouldn't support the SNP actually returned volumes of unexpected support in canvassing results. By the middle of March, he was convinced that the SNP were ahead of Labour, and that they could actually win the seat. If the SNP could turn out the vote, it looked like Aberdeen South could well elect him as their next MP.

On the day of the General Election the plan to get the SNP's vote out had been going well. By about nine o'clock in the evening Callum had stopped campaigning, and leaving the final hour to his election agent, he headed to his mum's for a rest before the exit poll came in. First, though, he stopped off at Aberdeen council's headquarters to hand in his resignation from the council: 'I had decided I was not going back... so I resigned my council seat at 22:50, just before the close of polls.' During the campaign Callum had felt that it was time to move on from the council and hand over to someone new; not wanting to make it a campaign stunt he chose to do it just before the close of polls so that, win or lose the election, he knew where he stood.

The next three hours were excruciating: exit polls declared that at least one SNP member wasn't going to be elected. He had given his election agent strict instructions not to call until he could give an indication of the result: 'I was looking at Twitter and everyone was saying that Aberdeen North looked comfortable and Aberdeen South was too close to call.' It wasn't until 00:15 that his agent and Kevin Stewart telephoned. 'Too close to call,' they said. 'They thought we were ahead but they couldn't be sure... but by the time I had got to the count, they were confident we'd won the seat.' Callum went on to win a majority of over 7,000 votes, seeing a swing to the SNP of just less than 20%. This result meant that, for the first time ever, both the city's MPs – and all of the city's constituency MSPs – were from the SNP.

8. EILIDH WHITEFORD
BANFF AND BUCHAN

Eilidh Whiteford was born in Aberdeen in 1969 and raised in the small fishing town of Macduff in Banffshire. While the town didn't have the amenities commonplace in cities, she loved the freedom that living in rural Scotland provided: 'It gave me an identity,' she said of her hometown. Rural and situated on the coast, Macduff provided her with the ability to remember 'more than just tower blocks': her childhood was filled with open fields and the sight of shipping boats returning home with the day's catch. It wasn't until later that she truly grew to appreciate the town: 'It was a great place to grow up, but I wanted something a little bigger when I was younger,' Eilidh recalled. The chance to experience this came when she was accepted into the University of Glasgow to study a degree in English and Scottish Literature. Before leaving Macduff, however, she had a chance encounter with a young man seeking election to the UK Parliament: Alex Salmond.

Eilidh's father had been a supporter of the SNP since the early 1960s, but she was unconvinced until she met Salmond: 'I just wasn't sure about the SNP when I was in my teens... but this young guy Alex Salmond convinced me to give them a hearing.' As the 1987 General Election approached, just months before leaving Macduff, she became heavily involved in the surging local SNP campaign that saw Salmond elected to the House of Commons, beginning the transformation of the seat from a Conservative Party bastion into an SNP stronghold.

Leaving Macduff for Glasgow so soon after the SNP's General Election victory had inspired Eilidh and convinced her that the SNP was the right party for her. Instead of focusing on her university classes she became a major part of the Federation of Student Nationalists (FSN), later becoming President in 1989, and campaigning with the organisation across Scotland for the SNP.

In her final year of university she discovered a passion for the academic study of Scottish literature. While she had always enjoyed it, campaigns had taken first preference over university work until this point. In her final year, as she began to focus, she realised how enjoyable academia had been for her. It was then that one of her lecturers, seeing the passion Eilidh had for the subject, suggested that she consider the idea of studying for a Masters degree abroad: 'He was Australian, so talked me into looking at studying somewhere international rather than in Scotland. Which as crazy as it seems now was the first time I had ever seriously considered leaving Scotland.'

After graduating with a first class honours degree in English and Scottish Literature, Eilidh moved to Canada to study for a Masters at the University of Guelph, before returning to the University of Glasgow to study for a PhD on the work of the author Alasdair Gray. Halfway through her PhD however, she came to the conclusion that a lifetime in academia was not for her: 'What I really wanted to do was get back into the political environment with an NGO [...] I really wanted to effect some meaningful change, and I didn't see that happening as an academic.'

'After finishing my PhD I approached Allan Macartney about the potential of working for him [...] luckily he found a job for me doing admin work, but that meant I could move back up to the North East,' she later recalled. Following his death in 1998, Eilidh went to work for Allan McCartney's successor, Ian Hudghton. Shortly after working on the 1999 European Election campaign, Eilidh left working with the SNP to once again return to the University of Glasgow, to lecture in Scottish Literature in the department of adult learning.

Yet throughout working with the party and the University of Glasgow, Eilidh still hoped to move into working for an NGO: 'It was really hard trying to convince people that I wasn't just an egghead with a PhD,' she joked. It was a frustrating time for her, but a break came in 2001 with the offer to join Carers Scotland: 'They were trying to provide an umbrella organisation for children's, carers, and disability organisations to lobby around the Community Care (Scotland) Bill [...] so I got the chance to coordinate that response to that bill on carers' rights.' Her time at Carers Scotland marked her entry into the voluntary sector: 'I was very very thankful for Carers Scotland giving me that break.'

When she finished work on the Community Care (Scotland) Bill, she was offered a dream job working for Oxfam in Scotland: 'I had very much grown up as part of the Live 8 generation, so it was the perfect job!'. She was brought in as a Policy and Public Affairs Officer, and immediately became a key part in the Make Poverty History Campaign: 'I still look back on it as one of the proudest days of my life, when 250,000 people marched through Edinburgh. People came from all over the world for the march, but most of the people that came were from around Edinburgh. We worked so hard to make it happen and we couldn't believe how many people showed up. But for me I was really proud that Scotland showed up.' She stayed with Oxfam following the Make Poverty History campaign, becoming the organisations, Scottish Campaigns Manager while working some of Oxfam's African programmes.

In 2007 Eilidh started to look for a new challenge. It was then that Stuart Pratt, the longtime election agent of Alex Salmond, spoke to her about the possibility of running for parliament as a successor to Alex: 'I didn't say no, so the next day Stuart had sent the nomination forms to my inbox.' Standing for parliament was always something that Eilidh had considered, but it was something that always seemed like a step for the future. Wanting to get real life experience first, she had resisted earlier calls to stand for the Scottish Parliament. The opportunity to stand as Alex Salmond's successor came at just the right time for her, 'so I decided I would go for it'.

She was selected in 2007, and it was assumed that there would be an election later on in the year. However, it turned out to be Gordon Brown's election that never came: 'I felt in a kind of limbo experience,' she recalled. Over the next two years Eilidh still worked full-time with Oxfam on weekdays and at weekends she returned to Banffshire to campaign in the seat: 'It was a really difficult time, so I left my job a year [before] the election and moved back into my parents' house in Macduff, which allowed me to campaign full-time.'

Eilidh won her seat in 2010: despite a swing away from the SNP, she claimed over 40% of the vote in her constituency. Going down to London and working in Westminster was a bit of a culture shock: 'It was difficult just getting around. There are about 6,000 people on the estate, which is about twice the size of the town I grew up in.' The shock of Westminster wouldn't deter her however, and by the election of 2015 her constituency would return her with the second largest share of the vote for any Scottish MP, despite the area heavily voting No in the Referendum.

9. BRENDAN O'HARA
ARGYLL AND BUTE

Brendan O'Hara was born in Dennistoun in 1963. After holding his newly born son, his father announced to his family that he was going to call him Brendan but his grandmother's response was swift: 'Charlie, don't call him that. He'll never get a job'.

Brendan was raised in Dennistoun. Then known as 'Spam valley', he considers himself to have been raised in a working-class area filled with aspiration: 'I have no stories of poverty or desperation,' he recalled. 'I had a fantastic childhood and looking back Dennistoun was a great place to grow up. [...] There were always hundreds of kids playing football on the streets or chicky melly. I loved growing up.'

Although he paints a glorious childhood, he hated school more than anything. Treating it more as a social club than a place for learning, he preferred to believe that he could learn by osmosis rather than partake in actual studying. After leaving school he went straight into work with Strathclyde council's housing department.

During this time he became heavily involved in the SNP. His father was an Irish nationalist who, according to Brendan, 'made the very sensible leap into becoming a Scottish Nationalist as well'. While his father never forced his ideals onto his son, Brendan grew up knowing what he believed in: Scottish independence. His first involvement with the SNP was during the 1982 Hillhead by-election that would see the SDP's Roy Jenkins elected to the House of Commons while the SNP poll came in fourth on 11%. Despite that, Brendan would join the party on polling day as an act of belief in the cause: 'The SNP was going nowhere as a party back then, but I knew what I believed in so the SNP was the only party for me.'

Unenthused by his work with Strathclyde council, Brendan threw himself into the SNP. He stood as a candidate in the 1984 and 1986 council elections, and at the age of twenty-four, he stood as the party's candidate for Glasgow Springburn. He was the youngest candidate at that General Election. Losing each time, as he knew he would, his experiences with the SNP started to change his character. Working for the council's housing department wasn't enough and he decided that going back into education was the only option.

At college, Brendan achieved all the Higher results that he needed and was accepted to study a Bachelor's degree at the University of Strathclyde in Modern, Social, and Economic History. 'I loved it,' he declared. 'It was the most incredible four years of my life. To be given a grant to just read was incredible.' His chance to experience the world of work before going to university, he believed, stood him in good stead: returning to education all those years later, he had a different understanding of what education was all about.

Leaving university in 1992, Brendan landed a trainee journalist post with the *Catholic Observer*, a position that his mum had spotted and had convinced him to apply for. He then moved onto a job with the politics team at STV. From here, a dream vacancy arose in the sports team. Brendan speculatively applied for it, not expecting to get the position, but as it turned out he was the perfect in-house candidate. He was quickly offered the job, working to produce much of STV sports coverage: 'I must have been doing a good job with the sports team, as after about a year working there I got a phone call and was asked to go to South Africa to cover the Rugby World Cup.' The chance to cover the event, so soon after the fall of the apartheid regime, was 'one of the greatest experiences of my life'.

Soon after getting back from South Africa, Brendan married and started to think about settling down somewhere in Scotland long-term. However, following on from the Rugby World Cup, he received a phone call from Sky Sports offering him the chance to move to London in an assistant producer's role. He couldn't turn it down, but promised his wife that they would move back up to Scotland at the first chance.

From this point, Brendan dropped out of active engagement with the SNP but remained a passionate supporter of the party. Having moved to London at the tail end of 1995, it was not possible to heavily campaign for the party during the important years of the devolution Referendum and first Scottish Parliament elections. In 2000, he finally returned to Scotland to work for BBC Sport as he had promised to do, yet the birth of his young daughters held off his thinking of standing again for electoral politics: 'My daughters were born in 2002, and I decided not to stand for parliament because I had a young family and it wouldn't have been fair to them.'

Brendan finally moved out of sport in the early 2000s, after winning an award for his team's documentary on Bosnia's first international football match as an independent country against Scotland. He then started working with the BBC's comedy team on productions like Comedy Connections, which he continued to do until 2009 when he decided to set up his own production company: 'We did a lot of work with STV, such as *The Football Years* and *Road to the Referendum*, which were both BAFTA nominated.'

Following the Referendum, Brendan was devastated at the outcome of the result. 'I thought – I have to do something – so the Referendum defeat was really the catalyst for deciding to run.' After his wife and daughters had agreed to the decision, Brendan stood for the SNP in his home constituency of Argyll and Bute. On paper, the seat was a four-way marginal between the major parties, but Brendan believed it was a race between the Tories and the SNP: 'I always believed that the Liberals were seen as the best bet to keep the Tories out, and once they had decided to go into coalition with the Tories they couldn't claim that mantle anymore.'

The campaign was fought over one of the UK's largest constituencies, and early on, the SNP worried that it could have been a seat targeted by a tactical voting campaign. The campaign was however dominated by the massive SNP ground effort across the constituency, but it wasn't until the night at the election count that Brendan started to think that he might win: 'We were all waiting for Helensburgh,' he said. 'As the constituency's major urban area and a traditionally strong area for the Liberal Democrats, it would likely be a telling point of just how well the SNP were doing.' As the boxes were being counted, Brendan waited nervously for enough sampling to come back to give a fair idea of how the campaign was going. It wasn't until early in the morning that O'Hara knew how Helensburgh had played out, but when the sampling was concluded, the SNP had almost beaten the Liberal Democrats in the total number of votes. At this point O'Hara became convinced the SNP would win the seat.

His victory constituted the first time that Argyll and Bute had elected an SNP MP since the historic election of 1974 when the party won eleven seats. When the result in Argyll and Bute was finally confirmed as the fifty-fifth seat that the SNP had won that night, Brendan, ecstatic about the election, thought about the members of the SNP who had campaigned for him back in 1987 and who had sadly not lived to see this election. Brendan explained: 'What we have to remember is that we are standing on the shoulders of giants. People have dedicated their lives to this cause in full knowledge that they would never be remembered. When the history of the movement is written there will be many many pages dedicated to Nicola and Alex, but there will be no pages dedicated to Jimmy Williamson, Malcolm Grahame, and Alex Livingston. But without the Jimmys and Alexs there would never have been a book to write. It was them who had kept our movement's flame burning in the dark dark times, and we should always remember that.'

10. PAUL MONAGHAN
CAITHNESS, SUTHERLAND, AND EASTER ROSS

One of the many academics in the 56, Paul Monaghan did not take the traditional route into academia. He was born in Montrose before moving to Inverness at the age of two. Attending Inverness Royal Academy where he describes himself as 'not a very good pupil', from the age of twelve, Paul's main interests were cars and motorbikes. With an ambition to work in a garage, this is exactly what he did at the age of sixteen when he left school. After eighteen months of working as a panel beater, Paul decided that he wasn't suited for the work and instead accepted a job in social care.

After some time, Paul decided he wanted to get some qualifications and he enrolled at Stirling University to study for a degree in Psychology and Sociology. Achieving a first class degree, one of his lecturers then approached him to ask if he would consider doing a Masters degree in the department. Paul attended an interview for a bursary for the Masters course and he was invited to apply for a PhD instead.

Paul's area of study focused on the role of the board of social responsibility in the development and implementation of social work policy in the post-war period. He won funding from the Economic and Social Research Council, who were looking to create a research partnership between the University of Stirling and the Church of Scotland's board of social responsibility. Paul was awarded his PhD in 2004, at which point he was working for the police as Head of Planning and Development for the Northern Constabulary: 'This was a very interesting role about strategy, policy, putting in place operational plans. At that time the police service were also being driven to think about performance management systems and all of that.' After a few years in that job Paul decided to go back into social care and became Director and General Manager of a charity called the Highland Homeless Trust.

Paul explained how his political interests started during childhood: 'I come from a family that aren't particularly political, but for as long as I can remember I've always been interested in politics. I've always been interested in the organisation of society and how it's structured and governed. From a very early age, I think I bemused my parents by always questioning why Scotland was governed from London, which was clearly in a different country. Even to this day I struggle with this concept, and I've consistently believed that Scotland should be a sovereign nation and a self-governing nation in its own right, which is what I'm working towards now.'

Paul first joined the SNP in 1994 although he said he would 'never, ever have joined any other party because I disagree with the ideology of some of them, I disagree with the approach that others have, and I fundamentally disagree with the objective that all of the other parties have which is the fact that Scotland should be governed from London.'

Before being elected as MP Paul held positions within his local branch as well as founding 'Yes Highland', which campaigned across the Highlands for a Yes vote in the 2014 Scottish independence Referendum. As he was so involved in the Yes campaign, I asked Paul whether the No result was particularly difficult to deal with: 'I think it was a hard blow. More than that though it was plain disappointing. I get disappointed when I hear fellow Scots talking Scotland down and suggesting that somehow we're better off being part of the United Kingdom and I think it's plain to see that we're not better off. As a nation we suffer in all sorts of different way from being governed down here. I think the economic case for Scottish independence is unassailable. I think that even a cursory glance over the facts show that in financial terms, in social terms, and in demographic terms, we would be better governed independently, and that's what we should shoot for. I think increasingly the people of Scotland hold that view and the stories and the promises of the No side are shown to be misrepresentations at the very least and falsehoods probably more accurately.'

Sitting in Westminster, one of the main focuses for Paul is tackling the Tories' austerity agenda: 'I fundamentally disagree with the Westminster government's austerity agenda. I don't believe there is a nation ever in history that has recovered from a financial crisis by implementing cuts. A great hero of mine was Franklin Roosevelt – the only four-term President of America. On election in the 1930s he really addressed the great depression and took America from the depths of despair with citizens facing significant hardship and impoverishment. He took them from that situation to the US being the most powerful nation the world has ever known within a relatively short period of time. Roosevelt didn't do this by cutting, he did this by investing in people [...] by providing people with opportunities to grow and develop and prosper. That is exactly what I believe should be happening in the UK now, and [it is] certainly what should be happening in Scotland just now. It would be happening in Scotland if we could implement economic policy relevant to Scotland.'

Speaking in London, Paul described how the views of people in his constituency and Scotland are generally far removed from those in England: 'They don't just have different political views but also a different culture. I think not only the political views in Caithness and Easter Ross are different to the views down here, I think a lot of people down here would consider my constituency to be an alien environment and I think that my constituents would perhaps consider down here to be an alien environment as well. [...] One of the key differences that I've noticed since being down here is that the people in my constituency are very welcoming of outsiders. They hope to see people to live in the constituency that can bring new skills, aspirations, and experiences and also contribute their culture to that part of the world. It's a very inclusive society. What I see down here is a society that wants to build barriers, to exclude people, that wants to restrict and impose restrictions on others. It's very, very different indeed. We can see that in the EU Referendum bill, where they are restricting voting – not wanting sixteen- and seventeen-year-olds to vote – but also EU nationals despite opening it up to people of the Commonwealth.'

'I think there is a very good chance that the UK as a whole will vote to leave the EU. There is a significant momentum for that down here. I don't think there's feeling for it in Scotland at all really. I think Scotland has a long history of involvement with European nations, which is different here. In fact, manifestly different. I think if the UK votes to leave the EU the results would be negative and significant for us. I think that would represent the material change that Nicola Sturgeon mentioned would be required before another Referendum on independence.'

When asked what he would like to see in a future, independent Scotland, Paul replied: 'I want to see a Scotland that is socially just, I want to see a fairer Scotland. I want to see a Scotland where we invest in people, where our education system is invested in, where our right to free education is extended and sustained. As a people we are historically inventive and creative and we have been responsible for some of the great innovations that have taken us to where we are as a highly technological species. I don't just want to see Scotland prosper but have an international focus and be outward-facing and inclusive. The only way we can achieve all of that aspiration is independence.'

11. DREW HENDRY
INVERNESS, NAIRN, BADENOCH AND STRATHSPEY

Andrew Hendry was born in 1964 in Edinburgh, and not long afterwards he became known as Drew. He was brought up in a council house and his father had been a painter and decorator who, at his own expense, put himself through college to become a teacher. At the age of nineteen, shortly after leaving high school, Drew decided to set up his own mobile disco business; it would never rake in big money but it paid for all the petrol and records he wanted. Before long, he got a job working on the shop floor at Currys and worked his way up the company's management scheme. His dad's drive to get to where he wanted to be provided a constant inspiration and motivation for Drew to reach the top, whatever he chose to do.

Eventually, Drew transferred into the manufacturing sector and joined the company AEG: 'There I was their Regional Sales Manager for Scotland; that term used to bug me even then. Then I become the National Sales Manager for the UK, which *really* bugged me,' he joked. Continuing with this career, Drew became a director of Electrolux, before deciding to set up a digital marketing company. Having dreamed of living in the Highlands since visiting Loch Ness as a young boy, he decided to move 'lock, stock and barrel up to Inverness' in 2003 to start his company.

In Inverness, Drew scouted out the right premises and people to make his new business a success. 'However, it was only when I arrived [that] I realised that the infrastructure wasn't there to support us,' he recalled. 'There was not Internet connection, and it was a real panic and problem. I had to buy expensive ISDN lines just to keep the business going. This was an early indication of how far behind we were, which I felt had to change.'

Drew had been a supporter of the SNP since seeing the political actions of Labour and the Conservatives during the 1979 Devolution Referendum as an 'affront to democracy'. He started to work with the party because he saw that, if businesses like his were ever to become successful, things needed to change in the Highlands. In the end, his frustration with the Lib-Lab Scottish Executive convinced him to run for the council in 2007.

Elected in 2007, Drew argued passionately for more money to improve the infrastructure of the Highlands. Eventually, after the 2012 elections, he formed the first ever SNP-led Highland administration and became the council leader. At this point he never had any intention of running for either the Scottish or Westminster Parliament: while he was a passionate supporter of independence, the main reason Drew was in elected politics was to try and advance the Highlands. After the defeat in the Referendum his thinking began to change about what position he could best do this from: 'A lot of us [...] had a simultaneous spark [...] The promises that were made were very clear, and there was a responsibility for the Westminster parties to be held to that.'

Drew decided to run against the Liberal Democrats' most senior Scottish MP, Danny Alexander, planning to take him to task over his record of delivery for the Highlands. Many people regarded the seat as one that the Liberal Democrats could easily keep hold of. While the Ashcroft Polls suggested a landslide victory for the SNP, a result they would predict almost spot on, it wasn't until five days before the election that Drew began to think that it was going to be a fantastic result: 'Nicola Sturgeon was in Inverness and a spontaneous crowd arose,' he recalled. 'Nicola Sturgeon and I standing on a fruit crate in the middle of Inverness at the bottom of the Market Steps, and this crowd just forming around us. The fact we both went through the crowd taking selfies just captured the spirit and gave us a real indication of where we were going.' The day of the election was the most nerve-wracking experience of his life. Drew's family had been out all over the constituency campaigning on polling day as 'Team Hendry', looking to make sure that as many SNP supporters got to the vote as possible.

On the night, the result was sensational, seeing the SNP secure over 50% of the vote and gaining a 10,809 majority over the Liberal Democrats from being a distant third in the previous election. In his victory speech he called the election a 'new dawn' for voters, saying that 'it had been their night' and that people wanted an end to the harmful austerity dogma of the Conservative Party and a raft of progressive policies put in its place.

As a young teenager, Drew watched Scotland vote Yes in the 1979 Referendum yet still be denied a Scottish Parliament. For Drew, therefore, the General Election was a long-awaited reaction, which made him think of the many people he had seen vigorously campaigning for a party that might have never broken through. But the SNP had that night: 'I am always aware of the old phrase, 'standing on the shoulders of giants'. I know that I wouldn't be here today if it hadn't been for the work of the people during the 1979 campaign and the future campaigns. We all carry with us a great sense of responsibility, that we do the right thing to repay all those people who invested so much over so long.'

12. ANGUS ROBERTSON
MORAY

Angus Robertson is the leader of the SNP group in what he calls the 'parallel universe' of Westminster. He holds the honour and responsibility of coordinating Scotland's 56 SNP MPs, and ensured that they got off to a flying start in 2015. Angus had been preparing for a victory though he 'did not foresee 56 of 59'. He comments: 'in the run up to the election something became pretty clear to me that hadn't been noticed at the time – all of the opinion polls were indicating it would be likely that the SNP would be having more seats than the Lib Dems. People were all asking 'Will it be twenty? Will it be thirty?' and so on, and although the figure was unknown, it was clear it was going to be quite a lot. If we were to become the third party in the House of Commons, that would have an impact on things because of the role of precedent. I started having conversations with parliamentary authorities about what that would mean, so there was a lot of thinking about what we would get and be responsible as a new SNP group.'

Angus's swift and careful preparation meant that, almost immediately after the General Election, measures were in place for all the new MPs. 'The other thing I did was meet with each of the [other] 55 MPs and speak with each of them about their backgrounds, needs, interests, concerns, and expectations, and I worked hard to build the group on solid foundations. Each MP has been assigned to a policy group.'

Now a talented parliamentarian and a clearly passionate group leader, Angus started life in Wimbledon in 1969 before moving with his parents to Edinburgh at the age of one. He attended Broughton High School which he 'very much enjoyed', getting involved in many areas across the curriculum including musical activities like playing the violin for the Edinburgh Secondary Schools' Orchestra. Not only involved in classical music pursuits, he played other instruments as well including the bass guitar and he played heavy rock music with friends. Young Angus Robertson also enjoyed sport, playing for Broughton FP Rugby Club and The Grange Cricket Club: ' a little known fact is that cricket is played more than rugby in Scotland, you know.'

Angus also became politically active while at school. He talked about when he first started to engage with politics: 'I remember listening to the radio in the run up to the 1983 election and I must have been about twelve. It was an interview with someone from the SNP and I was interested in the fact there was a Scottish political party, though I remember thinking the style of the interview was quite aggressive and that the person on the radio wasn't being treated particularly respectfully. In that same year I kept an SNP lamppost poster from the election and put it up on my wall.'

With a Scottish father and German mother, Angus was brought up bilingually and remembers speaking German to his grandmother who lived with the family at that time. He recalled a story his father told him about an early political experience: 'My father told the story of coming back home and telling my granny that while I was uptown on Princes Street there had been an SNP stall or event and I was explaining to my granny I had met 'Herr Wolf' (with a very pronounced 'v') who was Billy Wolfe – so it translated neatly!'

Angus also explained how growing up with the backdrop of the Thatcher era affected the politics of his peers: 'It's curious now because when I have followed my friends, people I knew at school, my generation almost without exception are all Yes voters and many are SNP members. There must be something about that experience in the 1980s of Margaret Thatcher being in, when we didn't vote for the Tories and what was happening to Scotland at the time. [...] There was a bit of a cultural renaissance as well if you think about all the Scottish bands that were on the go in the 1980s and if you think about the fact that there were Scottish films that were cool. There was a bit of confidence going on so it felt entirely natural for me to want to get involved in the SNP.'

The story of Angus joining of the SNP is also particularly noteworthy. After thinking about signing up for the party for a while, Angus found a membership form lying in the street: 'maybe it was fate [...] thinking back it does seem very odd.' He filled it out and sent in an application to join the youth wing of the SNP, the YSN. Then, 'a tall guy with glasses came to the front door and signed me up. I now know him as Charlie Reid, who then hadn't – along with his brother, Craig – made his breakthrough as The Proclaimers. He signed me up in 1985 and then I started going to YSN meetings and got involved with the SNP and I went along to all kinds of meetings and by-elections and that was the start and I never looked back!'

After Angus joined the party aged fifteen he got involved with some memorable campaigns: 'Shortly after becoming involved I would help out in the SNP's Headquarters which was then on North Charlotte Street, so I would help out repairing the SNP research department bulletin, helping with the press cuttings. I remember being one of the people that volunteered on the night of party political broadcasts because people would be encouraged to join, so they needed us to sit and man the phones to accept new members.'

'I did all that as a sixteen- and seventeen-year-old and at that time this impressive, young, aspiring politician by the name of Alex Salmond was around – I remember him asking me if I wanted to go and take part in his campaign in Banff and Buchan. This was in the run up to the 1987 General Election so I would have been seventeen then. I went up and stayed with the legendary election agent for Alex Salmond, Stuart Pratt. I remember sleeping in a room with a whole load of other students and young people helping with the campaign.'

'Shortly after [there was] the Govan by-election, so there's a whole generation of people in the SNP – I'm thinking of Richard Lochhead or Fiona Hyslop or Nicola Sturgeon – that all got involved at the same time and a lot of our experiences were around these by-election campaigns.'

Already with some experience of politics under his belt, Angus went to Aberdeen University to study Politics and International Relations and almost immediately after arriving got involved with student politics: 'I was elected to what was then called the SRC, the Students Representative Council of Aberdeen University, and I think I was the youngest SRC at the time which meant I had to carry the mason. There are some curiosities about that time and people that were involved at that time too: John Nicholson MP's brother was in the SRC with me, Alistair Carmichael was on the SRC at the same time as me. The SNP club AUSNA had, amongst their members, Kevin Pringle, who was in the year above me.'

After leaving university Angus headed to Vienna to spend some time teaching without much of an idea what he wanted to do. After a few months he had his first journalistic break via the Austrian magazine *Profile*: 'I remember writing this article and turning up at the editorial offices and asking to speak to the editor – I'm not even sure if I knew the name of the editor. It was by pure chance that [...] the foreign news editor was walking past and he had a look at the thing I had written and published it the next week. I was on a television programme in Austria a few years ago and this guy who gave me my big break was on the panel and I was able to say to him how appreciative I was of him giving me the understanding that it was possible to do this.'

Having been published in such a prominent magazine, Angus was given the opportunity to work for Blue Danube Radio, reporting on the ongoing conflict in former Yugoslavia. Around this time he was contacted by BBC Scotland about providing information on the conflict on the radio. What was supposed to be a year out of university on the continent turned into a decade of journalism with Austrian media, BBC Radio Scotland, BBC World Service, and then a TV programme called *Correspondent*.

Even though he was mainly working in Austria, Angus had returned to Scotland regularly to help with elections. The 1997 election made him think seriously about returning to politics; at this time he was working in SNP Headquarters managing the international press: 'I remember thinking to myself that I would have regretted not being part of that historic first election for the Scottish Parliament, so I gave up my job and flew back from Vienna for vetting and began to understand selection proceedings and how all of that might work. I put myself forward for the 1999 election in Midlothian.'

After failing to gain Midlothian in the Scottish elections, Angus started working with the Scottish Parliament for the SNP group on European and International affairs. Shortly thereafter in 2000 he was selected to be the SNP candidate for Moray, as the incumbent SNP MPs had all declared that they were going to concentrate on the Scottish Parliament.

Angus spoke about his decision to pursue a career in Westminster: 'I have always had such long-standing interest in foreign affairs and defence matters. There is a huge attraction about being in the Scottish Parliament in Scotland, but given that the Scottish Parliament doesn't control those things that I have had an expertise and interest in I thought that there was a role to be played. From 2001 I became the foreign affairs spokesperson for the party which I have been for nearly fourteen years now, and I was always very clear in making the case for the role that Scotland could play in any international affairs and defence context.'

Angus served as the SNP Campaign Director for the 2014 Scottish Independence Referendum, which he described as 'all consuming'. Shortly after the elections in 2011 Angus visited Quebec to learn about what to do – and what to avoid – based on their experiences of the 1999 referendum on independence. He then returned and became very involved in promoting the grassroots Yes organisations.

Commenting on Westminster he stated: '[it] was and remains, in many respects, in a parallel universe. Speaking to English parliamentarians they had very little understanding of what was going on in Scotland. There was a sense of 'the restless natives will have their fun but they will come to their senses' and 'you have no chance' and none of them expected the Yes vote to be as strong as it was.'

When asked what he was like outside of politics Angus replied enthusiastically: 'I would like to think I'm alright!' He then went on to explain his continuing love of music by joking, 'I better not say too much as you might get the impression that I'm on retainer from Spotify.' He also enjoys watching football and as much rugby as he can and is an avid cook.

In their passionate visions for Scotland many of the 56 draw upon their past careers and interests. Describing a Scotland with an international focus, Angus is no different: 'I can't wait for Scotland to become independent again, confident, excited about opportunities, focused on the societal and economic challenges we have and [being] the most successful country we can be. I'm enthused about the role that Scotland can play in European and international affairs and play a positive peace-orientated role in regional and international defence and security. I think generations in the future will wonder why we didn't make the choice to be independent earlier!'

13. ANGUS BRENDAN MACNEIL
NA H-EILEANAN AN IAR

Angus MacNeil is an experienced SNP MP, having been elected in 2005 for the constituency of the Hebrides and Western Isles. Born on the Isle of Barra in 1970, he attended Castlebay Secondary School until the age of sixteen, when he moved to the Nicholson Institute on Stornoway. Clearly rooted in his constituency, Angus proudly stated that by the time he was seventeen or eighteen, he 'knew people from just about every village on every island in the outer Hebrides'.

Following secondary school, Angus moved to Glasgow to study Civil Engineering at Strathclyde University, which he didn't enjoy: 'University was nothing like school, it was a terrible place. I have no misty nostalgia about university at all.' After this Angus worked as an engineer and as a reporter for BBC Radio Scotland, before qualifying as a teacher in 1996 at Jordanhill College.

Despite growing up in one of Scotland's most remote constituencies, MacNeil was not estranged from political matters and he keenly followed international events on the family's television: 'We didn't get television until about January of 1980 when I was nine years old. I watched programmes like *World in Action* and *Panorama*, the news, and historical content such as Robert Keys' *A Television History of Ireland* and I found these very instructive. Programmes like *World in Action* and *Panorama* seemed to have budgets that went beyond what was happening north of the White Cliffs of Dover and went around the world to give a general worldview.' He also credits the fact that Thatcher was in power then and, with rising unemployment, there were many domestic social issues that pricked his conscience.

From this youthful interest Angus remained interested in politics but never active: 'I never went to an SNP meeting or any political meeting – that was a mistake. In 1987 I campaigned for Callum McDonald, the Labour candidate who I eventually beat in 2005. When I first voted it was for Labour in 1989, probably in the Glasgow Central by-election.' His switch to the SNP came between 1989 and 1991 when he campaigned for Brendan O'Hara who is now the MP for Argyll and Bute and shares an office in Portcullis House with Angus.

Angus blames his entry into politics on the 'Victor Meldrew syndrome'. 'I kept shouting at the television – I was told for a man of twenty-seven or twenty-eight years old [that] if I continued to do that I would develop blood pressure issues.' In 1998 he wrote a letter to a newspaper criticising Gordon Brown for saying that independence would make the sky fall in on the same week that Continental closed their tyre plant outside Bathgate in favour of one in Cork, a place more on the fringes of the British tyre market than the Outer Hebrides. After that letter, the SNP asked Angus to attend a meeting, which led to him later standing for election in 2001.

Since his election in 2005, Angus has caused a stir several times in Westminster. In 2006 he lodged a formal complaint with the Metropolitan Police regarding the Labour party's 'Cash for Honours' scandal. He and former MP Martin Bell wrote to the then-Prime Minister Tony Blair, calling for all appointments to the House of Lords to be suspended in the wake of the scandal. These actions lead to Angus being awarded Scottish Politician of the Year in November 2006.

When asked about how he felt after the Scottish Referendum result he gave an animated response: 'Oh, adjectives – crushed, gutted, disappointed, dispirited – I thought it was all over, didn't feel like anything good could ever happen again, thought that we were finished as a movement, thought that the dream had died, absolutely rock-bottom, aw heck what'll we do now, there's not a hope of us being back in Westminster, it's all over. Then, when Alex Salmond resigned I was going through Uist, by the site of the last battle with bow and arrows in Scotland, probably also the UK. Alex fired a couple of fantastic arrows himself into the air, which really struck home. The first was "think not how far short we fell of the summit but think of how high the base camp is for the next assault on the summit". The next thing he said was "the dream shall never die". While when I heard those words initially I thought they were just hopeful and dreamy, [but] when I met people in Castlebay on the Saturday evening I was the least nationalistic person that could be found in the Castlebay bar.'

Following his second re-election this year, Angus was made chair of the Energy and Climate Change Select Committee, the first SNP member to ever be appointed chair of an important Select Committee as a result of the resounding SNP victory in Scotland. Angus has a mixed focus this term in Westminster: 'most of my achievements and goals will be driven by the Select Committee now and there are many areas there. Equally, one of the important things in the manifesto is a link between the islands.' All these goals will be difficult, however, in a government that 'understands the price of everything and the value of nothing'. [...] We are ultimately controlled by a government who only has one MP in Scotland: these are the consequences of a No vote in the Referendum, it means these big decisions are out of our hands and the Tories can cut everybody. It's scarier than any scare story you heard before the Referendum. One thing you can say about the Referendum, though, is that it led to the election of the 56.'

Angus's pursuits outside of politics are closely tied with the island traditions of his constituency: 'I keep sheep, though I sometimes wonder if they are a hobby or another job. One of the things about them is that they probably keep you active as you have to do certain things with them at certain times, so it's like sheep will demand of you that you need to vaccinate them or give them certain medicines or you've got lambing to do and so on. [...] Another thing I like to work with is my boat – a seventeen-foot Fyvie Skiff. She was built in 1903 and was one of the vessels that took whisky off the Politician at the time of *Whisky Galore*. I restored her majorly in the 90s [...] I think she came to Barra first in the 1930s and I hope that she – Chrissy – will make it onto the sea this year and hopefully we'll see Chrissy sailing majestically around Barra.'

Angus's inspirations and ideological influences reflect both his political aptitude and island upbringing: 'It would be a toss up between Paulo Friere, who wrote the book *The Pedagogies of the Oppressed*, which I understand is a text for social workers, and the author Steven Pinker who wrote *How the Mind Works*. Steven Pinker made me realise in my twenties that the best piece of technology or kit you'll ever have is your own brain and it's what you do with it and how you use it that matters. Also, it taught me not to look up to anybody but not to look down at anybody either. Also, a little bit of Noam Chomsky's work.' On a more intimate level, however, Angus's inspiration was 'probably Mrs McCormack who was my primary teacher in the first four years – she had a great influence on my life as well, probably not as much as I realise or she realises – but most of my reference points to whatever is a lot of what she had said. Obviously my parents too!'

The vision Angus has for Scotland's future is one where many people can participate, a Scotland like the Scandinavian societies 'which will allow people to go to work, to see their full potential, have proper childcare, and have proper social security safety nets so that if you do fall on something unfortunate you're not discarded. I think we should have a society where people are valued – it sounds glib, but it's not – a society where people don't feel like they need to grab, grab, grab, as they know there is a safety net. I think a society that's Nordic, almost, in its outlook and isn't too individualistic – obviously you can't trample the right of the individual but the society does need to work collectively.'

'I also believe in a society where education is free, where healthcare is free, where pensions are reasonable, where childcare is there for those who need to go and work and pay taxes. In the UK we have childcare equivalent to the American healthcare system, very privatised and very inefficient and we could do better. Also, we don't need nuclear weapons. If we're talking about climate change [...] nuclear weapons will not lead to global warming but global frying, and I think that that is enough to be getting on with at the moment. We've all got our threescore year and ten on this earth and let's make it as decent and as happy as we can for all of us.'

14. IAN BLACKFORD
ROSS, SKYE AND LOCHABER

Ian Blackford was born in Edinburgh in 1961 and joined the SNP when he was just sixteen years old. In the run up to the first Referendum on devolution he had become convinced that Scotland was deserving of significant home rule and then eventually independence: 'I had nailed my colours to the mast,' he joked. Ian joined the party at a difficult time. Not long after joining, the SNP were defeated in both the devolution Referendum and then in the 1979 General Election, returning only two SNP MPs to the House of Commons. It was a dark time when doors were regularly slammed in his face at mere mention of the SNP: 'I had a passion for the SNP and more importantly for independence,' he said, 'and I think when you have that passion and belief that independence can bring about a better country, then that belief helped push you through the bad times.'

After leaving school Ian worked as a clerk in the Bank of Scotland at the age of eighteen, but he didn't see his future in the banking industry. He then had the chance to join the Edinburgh-based stockbroker Wood McKenzie before moving to London a few years later to become an analyst, and later fund manager, for an investment bank. The former chairman of Wood McKenzie is said to have told him that 'he left Scotland as a clerk and came back as a Chief Executive', referring to the fact that Ian would eventually rise to work in Deutsche Bank's operations in Scotland and the Netherlands in 1999.

While his career in the financial sector took off, Ian remained the same committed SNP supporter. He would, after twenty years of campaigning for the party, contest the seat of Ayr for the SNP in the 1997 elections and then a seat in the 1997 Paisley by-election, unsurprisingly losing both seats to the Labour Party. Ian had never expected to be a front-man for the SNP; as a long time treasurer of the party, he had always seen himself as a foot soldier to the cause of independence, and had felt that his best contribution to the party was from behind the scenes.

After leaving his position as treasurer of the SNP in 2000 and the financial sector in 2002, Ian and his wife moved to Skye to set up their own consultancy business in 2004. Moving to Skye had been something both he and his wife had considered for a long time: 'Both of us had a great affection for the place,' he said. 'My wife had been the SNP Group Leader on South Lanarkshire council and a Trade Union official. I had been an investment banker, and we decided we wanted to step back from those things [...] [taking] the view that we wanted to move to Skye.'

After moving to Skye, while still supporting the SNP, Ian's involvement with the party was reduced to being involved in the party's Skye branch. Instead his focus was on his consultancy business and on maintaining a small croft belonging to him and his wife. Once the Referendum became a reality, however, he became active once more in the SNP nationally and in the wider Yes movement. Ian was part of a pro-independence group that drafted a report on the future of banking for an independent Scotland, and in Skye, Ian took on a key organisational role for the local Yes campaign.

Despite the Referendum's crushing No vote, in Skye there was however a bittersweet sense of success. 'We voted Yes in Skye,' he said, 'I remember going to my next SNP branch meeting in Portree the Monday after the vote, and it was a wow moment for me. There was a sense of resolve at that meeting and it took me back. Soon then after a discussion with my wife and many others I decided that running in

2015 was something that I had wanted to do. I thought that I could contribute to the party.'

Supporting the party from behind the scenes was no longer an option. Soon selected as the party's candidate for Ross, Skye, and Lochaber, Ian had to contest the election against the former Leader of the Liberal Democrats, Charles Kennedy, who had held the seat for the party since he was twenty-three years old. The SNP needed a massive swing to win the seat, having finished a distant third in 2010. Ian took on his candidacy as a full-time occupation, trying to ensure that across the constituency the party had optimum organisation to effectively campaign everyone, and leave no voter without the opportunity to speak to someone from the SNP.

Having spent the day travelling across the constituency, Ian and his wife checked into a guesthouse on the night of the General Election, near to where the count was taking place: 'The feeling on the ground was pretty remarkable. The reception we were getting as we went round the constituency was really quite something to behold. You could see there was an enormous support for the SNP, but whether that would be enough to see us win the seat we weren't sure.' After the close of polls Ian returned to the guesthouse and waited to hear from his election agent: 'I was getting feedback from people at the count and around the country. We could tell it was going to be an amazing night for the SNP.' When Ian finally came into the count at about 1:30am it was clear that they would win the seat: 'I remember when I arrived at the count the first result I saw on the TV was Mhairi Black's declaration and that gave everyone an immense feeling and a belief that it was going to be unique night for the country.'

Ian won the seat – previously a long-standing Liberal Democrat stronghold – with a 24.9% swing towards the SNP and a majority of over 5,000. In his maiden speech to the House of Commons, he invoked the famous words of Donald Stewart, the first ever SNP candidate to win during a general election: 'If I stray into controversial matters, they will, in a sense, be impartial controversies, since as a Nationalist Member I shall be in controversy with both sides of the House from time to time. For that reason, if I stray I hope that it will be less objectionable to the traditions of the House.'

15. ANNE MCLAUGHLIN
GLASGOW NORTH EAST

Anne was born into a military family, and home, therefore, was never a set location. In the years after the Second World War and the Korean War, conscription was still a policy of the British Government. Young men who were medically fit had to serve in the military for at least eighteen months, and remain on the military reserves for at least four years more if they left. There was however a contrast to those that were called into National Service and those who joined voluntarily, as Anne explains: 'My dad sussed out that if you joined voluntarily you got paid 33% more than those who were called up for national service.' Born in Greenock, her mother had returned to her family home to give birth to Anne, while her father prepared their home in Netley, near Southampton, for his new baby daughter.

Anne was brought up in Netley before moving to Germany and then to other English cities. She had attended eight different primary schools before her father's job saw the family finally settle in Aldershot. While the move from place to place was a frustrating part of growing up, life in the military was an extremely enjoyable time for both Anne and her parents: 'My mum and dad loved the lifestyle, if not the politics. And the army in those days was really great with families. They took us on loads of family trips to see *Aladdin on Ice* and other shows.'

While the lifestyle was great, her father's disagreements with military politics often led to trouble with his superiors. Anne's favourite story recalls her father's disagreements with the military during Princess Anne's first wedding: 'Princess Anne was getting married. [The army] were all told a shilling would be taken out of their wages that month to pay for a wedding present. My dad dug his heels in, refused to pay, and all his seniors had words with him but he claimed that he was the only servicing member of the British Armed Forces not to contribute to Princess Anne's present.' While these stories were pleasing to the family, the actions of her father would put serious strain on his relationship with the military and in 1975, Anne's father finally decided to buy himself out. The family relocated to Greenock, before settling in Port Glasgow in 1976.

Port Glasgow was a radically different social experience for Anne. She recalled: 'almost every Monday morning it seemed somebody else in the class's dad had been made redundant because they all worked in the shipyards. If it wasn't their dads, it was their mums, who worked in the canteens or the shops or the pubs nearby. Soon there was nobody in my class [...] who had working parents, and it was really awful to watch that, those shipyards shrinking the way they did.' Fortunately for her, both her parents were now working as psychiatric nurses and there was no shortage of jobs in this area in Glasgow. Yet watching the dire economic situation in Glasgow at the time had a profound effect on her for years to come.

After high school Anne attended the Royal Scottish Academy of Music and Drama (RSAMD), but at the insistence of her father only on a part-time basis. She split her education between the RSAMD and the University of Glasgow, which ensured she would be both trained in acting but also have a bachelor's degree in Dramatic Studies. 'My dad couldn't believe [...] I wasn't going to become a lawyer and wanted to become an actress,' she recalls. But despite graduating with her BA she didn't go on to act, although she still hopes that one day she might get the opportunity to star in *Coronation Street*.

Instead, Anne joined the SNP at the time of the 1988 Govan by-election: 'I [...] was looking for something a bit more real than the world of acting. I went along to help, and I found Jim Sillars to be completely inspirational, and we won. So I got lulled into a false sense of security. I thought the SNP won things, and so I joined the party after the by-election.' Anne joined the party's Glasgow Central branch and was completely sucked into the campaigning nature of the SNP. After leaving her first branch meeting as the new Organiser, she was sent on a training weekend by the party to learn from Alison Hunter, the party's Director of Organisation: 'I just learnt so much from her, and became completely empowered,' she later said. Her new-found passion for the SNP led to her being first asked to stand as a candidate in the Strathclyde regional council election of 1990, and then as a candidate for the party in multiple elections thereafter. Through standing for the party in so many hopelessly unwinnable seats she gained the nickname 'Queen of the Unwinnables'. 'You knew you weren't going to win,' she said, 'but you have to give people the chance to vote SNP.' The nickname never bothered her, and neither did the fact she was never going win, because it wasn't about that: it was about espousing the principles of independence and the SNP.

By 2009 she finally had the chance to experience the end result of winning an election when she succeeded Bashir Ahmad on the Glasgow Regional List following his untimely death. She had never intended to be elected, and when it happened it was a shock to her system. However the experience would be short-lived, when again in the 2011 election, she took up the most difficult seat in Glasgow. Despite a huge swing towards the SNP in Glasgow Govan, she would still fall just over 2,000 votes short of winning the seat. 'I was so happy that we had won [nationally], but I was also really quite gutted after the Election.'

After the Election, Anne spent a few months working with the newly elected MSP for Clydesdale, Aileen Campbell; a temporary appointment until she had figured out what she was to do next. Having been invited to an event advertising the opportunity to volunteer in Sri Lanka, her next move was spontaneous: 'I walked through the doors knowing that I was going to love the idea [and] have a great evening. But I knew I would leave knowing that I would never set foot in Sri Lanka.' Within three months however she had worked her notice in

Aileen Campbell's office and by January 2008 Anne was in Sri Lanka.

Anne spent three months in Sri Lanka and found the whole experience 'incredible', but when she returned home to Scotland, reality set in. She had no choice but to sign on to a job centre employment programme, rendering her powerless; having to stick rigidly to the terms of her contract meant that she had to turn down opportunities to pitch business ideas to people, because she could face sanctions for not meeting quotas. It was a very dark time for her: 'A lot of people don't know that if I hadn't been elected I would have been in serious financial trouble,' she said. 'It wasn't why I stood for election and in fact the idea of standing made my mum really anxious. So I wasn't going to do it originally because I needed to focus keeping a roof over my head. But my partner was actually the one that talked me into it, because he thought I would have really regretted it if I hadn't.'

McLaughlin chose to run in the most difficult seat possible, with all polls suggesting that even with a massive national swing, the seat of Glasgow North East couldn't turn yellow: 'I thought that for us to win in Glasgow North East it had to be someone that really knew, lived, and had campaigned in the constituency for years. I felt I gave the party the best chance of winning in that seat.' On Election night, everyone still expected Glasgow North East's Labour MP Willie Bain to be re-elected. Canvass results had shown an amazing return for McLaughlin's campaign but they were going against all the polls. In the end, McLaughlin not only won the constituency, but achieved a record-breaking national swing of 39.3%.

Outside the terrace of the House of Commons, as 'Highland Cathedral' plays from a lone piper on Westminster Bridge, she reflects on the political journey that brought her to Westminster: 'My sister says [that] your thoughts create your reality. In 2007 when Alex Salmond announced he was to be First Minister of Scotland, the other parties could have stopped it. But he did it with such confidence that Labour and the Lib Dems were taken aback. From then on, as a party, we had the opportunity to govern and we proved ourselves.

People saw that we had taken away prescription charges and tuition fees, put those 1000 extra police officers on the street, saw that we had actually done something that made people's lives better. When they see their ballot paper now, I don't think they can bring themselves to vote against all those good things. It's our competent governance and ability to stand up for all of Scotland that I think has got us here.'

16. PATRICK GRADY
GLASGOW NORTH

Patrick Grady was born in 1980 in Edinburgh. His family lived there until he was three, then moved up to Inverness. Growing up in the Highlands under the governments of Margaret Thatcher and John Major, Patrick's parents were never shy to express distaste for the Conservatives. His parents, both Catholics, had raised Patrick to believe that while everything might not be good, there was a chance to solve injustices in the world.

Although these political ideas and values were ingrained, Patrick didn't immediately have an interest in politics. This was fostered by his high school Modern Studies teacher, as Patrick recalled: 'I remember being fifteen, and being taken to the Eden Court in Inverness. We were all at the top gallery watching this political speech.' The speech was by a recently elected Leader of the SNP, Alex Salmond, decrying the storage of nuclear weapons on the shores of Scotland. Witnessing the early speeches of Alex Salmond and other key figures of the SNP was a turning point for Patrick in his teens. Politics became a passion, and as this grew, his parents' values quickly became the foundations of his own political beliefs.

Patrick chose to attend the University of Strathclyde because he believed it to have the best Politics department in the country at the time. Enrolling in 1997, he got involved with the Federation of Student Nationalists and joined the SNP soon afterwards. The upcoming Referendum on the establishment of a Scottish Parliament was fast approaching, and Patrick was determined to play his part in the campaign. During this campaign, and the following campaigns for the Scottish Parliament in 1999, Patrick developed lasting friendships with many other students in the nationalist movement, including the future MSPs and Scottish Government Ministers Aileen Campbell and Jamie Hepburn: '[...] that 1999 campaign [...] helped establish us as friends but also established our politics,' he said.

Throughout university, while his interest in politics only deepened, Patrick fostered a real interest in the workings of international development. After university, and a one-year-long sabbatical to become the Student Union's President, Patrick accepted a dream role with the Scottish Catholic International Aid Fund (SCIAF): '[...] growing up in a Catholic household, you collect your money for SCIAF and you grow up learning that they are trying to fix the injustice in the world. So going to work for them was a huge privilege.' Working on campaigning and advocacy work for SCIAF was the perfect role for Patrick post-university: having spent almost his entire university career campaigning either for the SNP or in student elections, it felt like a natural next step. It was also here that he met a major influence on both his personality and his ideals: his first boss Mary Cullen.

Patrick was however determined to get field experience of working in a developing country: he wanted to see – and experience – how people in other countries lived. In 2004, following the end of his contract with SCIAF, he found an opportunity with the Scottish Church's World Exchange to travel either to India or Africa and work teaching children in a local community, he jumped at the chance: 'I always think how different my life could have been if I had gone to India. Malawi was, in the end, the obvious choice with its historic links to Scotland and the fact that I had always wanted to go to Africa.' Malawi was an insightful experience for Patrick. He had expected to visit a country with unmotivated and destitute people due to the poverty they were forced to live in. His experience changed his initial perceptions of life in the developing world forever: 'Life is the same everywhere,' he recalled. 'People were just going about their daily business, everyday living was different but people are just the same. Human beings are the same everywhere.'

After living in Malawi for one year, he decided to continue trying to expand his horizons outside of Scotland and took up a campaigning role with the Ramblers Association in London. While it was away from the work of international development, the role allowed him to return to a position that suited his skill set. Working in London did however mean that he missed out on the SNP's first national election victory in 2007, and afterwards the allure of returning home was too much to reject. He came back to Scotland and started working for Jamie Hepburn, one of the SNP's list MSPs for Central Scotland. It was also at the time that speculation started to emerge that then Prime Minister Gordon Brown would call an early General Election in 2007.

Patrick was unwilling to miss out on being involved in another major election for the SNP, so he put himself forward as a candidate for the Glasgow North seat on the rationale that, if selected, there would be a period of a few intense months of campaigning. Patrick was selected in late July as the SNP's candidate, but Gordon Brown never called the election: 'It is a really defining moment in recent political history,' Patrick contends. 'I thought we could have done quite well as it was just after we had gone into government at Holyrood, which I think that was the main reason that Brown bottled it.'

For the next two years Patrick, like the other candidates selected by the SNP, was on campaign alert in case Brown did decide to call a snap election. Rather than it being the few months he thought he would be campaigning for, he spent the next two years campaigning across the consistency of Glasgow North: 'It was a very intense period of campaigning,' he later admitted. When Brown finally did call the General Election in 2010, the results across Scotland would be an effective stalemate, with every constituency returning the same political party as they had done in the previous election. Patrick polled a disappointing third in Glasgow North, and felt burnt out after the election. Between working in the Scottish Parliament and campaigning, his life had been going at full speed for almost three years. Patrick needed a break and decided that he wouldn't try to run in the 2011 Scottish Parliament elections. 'After 2010 and that campaign I didn't feel up to standing in 2011,' he said.

Yet the burnout did not stop him getting heavily involved in the general campaign, and he became the election agent for Sandra White in the constituency of Glasgow Kelvin. After the victory of a majority SNP government and Sandra White in 2011, he decided to leave working for the SNP and move back into the charity sector, securing a position once again with SCIAF. This was not the end of his association with the SNP – he remained a member of the party and became the National Secretary in 2012 – but it was a conscious step back from the idea of forging his future in elected politics, and a return to his interest in international development.

After the defeat in the independence Referendum however, his thoughts began to change. As the dust started to settle after the Referendum and the General Election loomed, he decided that he had to throw his hat back into the electoral arena. Again, he would seek to contest the seat of Glasgow North, the seat that only five years previously saw him come in a distant third, behind both the Liberal Democrats and the Labour Party.

On Election night Patrick described the result as a 'reawakening' for the Scottish electorate. He claimed Glasgow North from the former Labour Scotland Office Minster Ann McKechin, and became the first ever SNP MP to be elected in a General Election for Glasgow. The result set the scene for Glasgow that night as each seat turned yellow. For Patrick the election was a justification of everything that had been said in the Referendum: people wanted a new voice for a new kind of politics in Scotland, and that is what they got.

17. ALISON THEWLISS
GLASGOW CENTRAL

Alison Thewliss was born in 1982 in the beginnings of Thatcherite Britain: the Falklands War was over, the Conservative Party was still a force in Scottish politics, and the SNP, in contrast, had recently suffered its biggest electoral setback in its forty-five-year history. Born in Lanark to two schoolteachers, the idea of a career in politics was a distant forethought for a young woman in the rural parts of Scotland: 'Growing up in Carluke, it was pretty quiet. Lot of fields to play in and climb trees.'

In her final years at high school, Alison began to be inspired by politics. In 1999 a local hustings was held in her school in the run up to the first Scottish Parliament elections and there was a feeling of excitement surrounding the whole process: 'We had speakers from all the political parties that came to the school and the SNP speaker had talked about the idea of building a fairer Scotland through independence. I thought there and then that it was the SNP I wanted to get involved in.' Aged seventeen, Alison joined the SNP, becoming part of a generation that now finds itself in the Houses of Power across Scotland and the United Kingdom.

By the Millennium, Alison had left Carluke to study Politics and

International Relations at the University of Aberdeen. Politics was now a passion for Alison, who was motivated by the idea that independence could bring about a fairer Scotland. Political campaigning quickly became almost part of her day-to-day routine. 'I just got absorbed into campaigning with Kevin Stewart,' she remarked on her days with the University of Aberdeen's Nationalist Society, AUSNA. Kevin Stewart, who would later become the MSP for Aberdeen Central in 2011, had always corralled the young talent of Aberdeen's academic institutions and helped develop them as future campaigners for the SNP. 'I loved campaigning,' Alison recalled. 'At a time we didn't have any MSPs or MPs in the city, so it was a bit of a slog [...] but it was a good introduction. Despite that the branch had no money, everyone was just mucking in and I loved that.'

Alison left university in 2004, hoping to find a role within the SNP. However, the 2003 Scottish Parliamentary elections had been a disaster, and this was later compounded by a difficult European election and the resignation of the party's leader John Swinney in 2004. 'It was a hard time for us and there was not a lot [of jobs] going so I moved back home with my parents and got a transfer from the Next retail shop in Aberdeen to one in Hamilton.' The opportunity to work for the party she loved didn't seem to be on the horizon, so Alison had to cast her net wider, and finally landed an internship abroad: 'I got an internship working for the Committee of the Regions in Brussels for three months. It was unpaid, but all the money I had saved up from working over the summer allowed me to do it.' Although this was a risk and a challenge, it seemed to be worth it: for the next three months Alison worked alongside delegates from across Europe's local government. Working with mayors from large German districts to local politicians of Greek Islands, it felt far removed from the reality of life in Scotland. Her campaigning days in Aberdeen led her to have a passion for 'doorstep issues', as she liked to call them, and European diplomacy and Brussels seemed totally removed from canvassing Aberdeen's high-rise flats. By the end of her internship Alison had a more concrete idea of the path she wanted to take, and back in Scotland, she secured a job as a caseworker with Bruce McFee, an SNP list MSP for the West of Scotland region. Moving to Glasgow, she found the role she'd been hoping for since leaving university in 2004.

Not long after starting with McFee in 2005, the crisis over the future of the Ferguson Shipyards arose concerning the future building projects of two Scottish vessels. Bruce McFee led campaigning to save the yard, leading Alison to also be intensely involved. While the campaign failed to overturn the Lib-Lab Scottish Government's decision to award a building contract to Polish shipyard Remontowa, the shipyard was saved by a multi-million pound ferry order from Caledonian MacBrayne. This was the first major campaigning success for Alison, and things gathered momentum from there.

As the elections of 2007 approached, Bruce McFee chose to stand down from his role as an MSP. Again the prospect of what to do next arose for Alison but this time fortune favoured her: backed by encouragement from across her local SNP branch in Kelvin, she ran for the council elections in Glasgow. The SNP claimed victory locally as well as nationally in 2007 and she became a Councillor for Calton. A heavy campaigning period followed for the SNP and for Alison, which saw the party gain another major victory against Scottish Labour Party in the 2008 Glasgow East by-election. For Alison and many other SNP supporters, the following four years seemed like the most successful period the party would ever see.

Alison's role as a councillor fitted in perfectly with her desire to help fix 'doorstep issues'. 'I loved being a councillor,' she said, 'It's that local ability for someone to phone you up with a problem, and you're able to be there in half an hour. I liked the ability to just be able to go and speak to people.' Re-elected in a close-run election in 2012, and then named as the party's spokesperson on Land and Environmental Services for Glasgow City Council, Alison could easily have been seen as a future parliamentary candidate. Yet her life was starting to settle nicely: she enjoyed her job, had recently married, and in 2010 she gave birth to her first child, a boy named Alexander, and in 2013, she had her daughter named Kirsty. Understanding that her life had changed with the arrival of a young family, she thought that her younger brother and father may have to find somebody else to cheer on Motherwell F.C. on game day.

Everything changed again, however, with the defeat in the

independence Referendum. 'I had no ambitions to stand as a parliamentary candidate,' she revealed. 'Then all the people started joining, and as branch secretary all my e-mails started pinging. I thought, something is happening here, something very strange and unexpected. I looked at all of these people that had made a bit of a leap in joining the party, and I thought maybe I should be doing something more. Then, there has been a lot of talk about getting other women involved, and I thought that if I don't step up myself how can I tell others to put themselves forward?'

Selected as the candidate for Glasgow Central, Thewliss had to go up against the Scottish Labour Party's own political dynasty and former Deputy Leader of the Party, Anas Sarwar. While Glasgow had voted for independence, the Glasgow Central constituency – in various boundary forms – had been held by the Labour Party since the 1950s and by the Sarwar faimily since 1997. Therefore, the likelihood of victory was always difficult for Alison to fathom: 'I hadn't expected to win the seat, because it was that seemingly unassailable majority.' Yet as the weeks and months rolled on things quickly started to change that hypothesis. She cheered gleefully. 'I kept expecting for there to be a bad canvass, and we went out to some of the most traditionally hostile areas and we would come back winning. I kept expecting some kind of indication to suggest it wasn't going to happen, but all our canvasses kept coming back really positive.' The party's canvass results were reaffirmed by an Ashcroft Poll showing the SNP taking 45% of the vote; it turned out that this had drastically underestimated the size of the SNP's and Thewliss's impending victory.

On election night Alison was there from 10pm counting the ballot boxes. 'I was right there from the start. I wanted to see it happening, to be a part of that.' As the ballots started rolling in it quickly became clear that both herself and the SNP were in for a good night in Glasgow, and she was surrounded by the young campaign team that had fought with her throughout the election. Her election agent Graeme Sneddon and friend David Linden had been managing expectations within the team, but as the night drew on, even the sternest face had to crack a smile. 'It was just the craziest night. In Glasgow you're used to going to the count and getting gubbed,' she said. Thewliss won her seat on a 27% swing from the Scottish Labour Party, meaning that all seven of Glasgow's Westminster seats had elected an SNP MP. Jim Sillars, former SNP MP for Govan – an area now covered by Alison – described the SNP's victory in Glasgow as 'Labour's version of the Walls of Jericho'.

Despite her enormous achievements, Alison maintains humble. Speaking in London she stated: 'I don't think you can stop being a normal person, and if you do that you lose why you have been sent here. You're here to do a job and represent Scotland, and that is what we need to remember. We can't get sucked into this ridiculous place with all its traditions. That is not why we are here.'

18. STEWART MCDONALD
GLASGOW SOUTH

Stewart Malcolm McDonald was born in 1986 in the Glasgow district of Castlemilk. Brought up in a working-class area with working-class parents, his parents both worked at the local school: his father is the janitor and his mother a cleaner. Despite the political battleground that Glasgow was, his household was never a debating chamber: 'There was no political background in my family,' Stewart explained. Life for his family wasn't about campaigning or marching down the streets. It simply was about getting through each and every day.

As a teenager, attending university was Stewart's ultimate goal. He aimed to study music and become a music teacher, but when the opportunity came to enroll he turned it down: 'For me it was a conscious choice,' Stewart stated. University at that point in his life just didn't seem like the right path to do down, and at high school he'd managed to get himself a job working in McDonald's which provided all that he needed: a wage.

After deciding not to attend university, the idea of working in McDonald's did however feel less appealing. He decided that he would study at Glasgow's College of Food Technology and look for employment in a more central location: 'I worked in the Marriott hotel, a zero hours contract, as a waiting staff member while at college.' His time in the food industry would be a short-lived experience, however, as he quickly realised that it wasn't an area that he wanted to stay in. Stewart moved into the retail sector, and it was here that politics first began to develop: 'My politics were entirely formed through actual experience, rather than joining a political club at university. Retail staff are incredibly under-paid, over-worked, not valued properly, and are often working in very poor conditions and long hours. When you go through that yourself, and that is your only source of income which is usually the minimum wage, you start to think surely we can treat people better.'

In 2006 Stewart joined the SNP, in part because of a lack of enthusiasm for any of Labour's front bench in Holyrood, and also due to the Iraq War, which had left the UK Labour party morally bankrupt in his eyes. He also strongly believed in independence. After joining the SNP he attended his first conference at the Glasgow Science Centre, with no real expectations of what it would be like. The opportunity to hear Alex Salmond and others articulate a vision for Scotland was not an opportunity he was willing to miss. In the end, he got more than he'd bargained for: by chance, the candidate looking to contest his local constituency, Nicola Sturgeon, invited him along to the SNP's next branch meeting. Excited at being asked by the party's Deputy Leader, he duly attended the meeting only to leave having been named the branch's Organiser. 'It was my first meeting, and I had no idea what an Organiser was. But I've never looked back.' This was the start of Stewart's political journey with the SNP.

With the 2007 elections nearing, the constituency of Glasgow Govan was a high priority for the party. This meant that the SNP's young new Organiser was heavily involved in trying to secure the SNP its first ever constituency MSP in Glasgow. While the SNP had been consistently ahead in the national polls since late 2006, the Labour party had held every Glasgow constituency since the formation of the Scottish Parliament in 1999. It was a year of constant campaigning for Stewart across the city, but it all paid off: his local constituency of Glasgow Govan was the first to elect an SNP MSP. Even though the Election was over, the campaigning didn't stop for Stewart.

Coming from a household where his father's politics were so radically different from his own – his father remains a unionist and monarchist – Stewart found it refreshing to talk and debate politics with people whose views mirrored his own. Eventually Stewart was hired as a caseworker for Anne McLaughlin, before moving to work for James Doran MSP after the 2011 Scottish elections. While the job as an MSP's caseworker was far from his earlier ambition of becoming a music teacher, it reinforced his reasons for being involved in politics. He passionately worked with people every day, many of them from a working-class background like himself who were struggling to make ends meet. 'Class and the class divide, that is what motivates me,' he later stated. 'People try to pretend it doesn't exist and it does exist. We are just given enough to tick us over. The imbalance of fairness, it is not tilted in the people of my background's favour.' The combination of anger and dismay at the class divide he witnessed on a daily basis ultimately convinced him to stand for the Westminster Parliament. However when he came to the decision to run in 2013, the idea of winning wasn't the goal. Instead he sought to talk about the issues of class and poverty, which he believed the Labour Party had abandoned. Yet after the Referendum everything changed.

The campaign was orchestrated by Kirsty McAlpine, a veteran of SNP campaigns, who served as Stewart's election agent. The idea for the campaign was that it would be completely community-based and that the constituency would ignore any national attention that it might get. When the first round of Ashcroft Polls came out, however, not just Glasgow South but the whole of Glasgow became an international story: despite the current Labour MP, Tom Harris, having a 12,000 majority, most media outlets were calling the seat a toss-up between the SNP and the Labour Party. The key moment in the campaign for Stewart wasn't the national polls or the massive rallies around Glasgow. It was the endorsement of a woman born and raised where it all began for him, in Castlemilk. Maureen Cope had been a supporter of the Labour party all her life: she had campaigned for the party, had leafleted for the party, and for decades, she had been relied upon to help get their voters out across Glasgow. For the first time, her vote rejected the Labour Party candidate and instead she publically endorsed Stewart, which he describes as 'a really good moment'.

On election night it wasn't just Maureen Cope that voted for him. Thousands of traditional Labour voters across Glasgow and Scotland cast their ballots one by one for the SNP. Stewart was the second last Glasgow MP to have his seat declared, but rather than nervously watching his ballots, he was able to cheer on his fellow candidates as result after result went to the SNP. 'It was amazing,' he recalled. Despite the polls, a mental barrier had existed in his mind: 'We had always sent Labour MPs to London. Always. And why would this time be any different?' he'd thought. As he cheered on his fellow candidates, he couldn't, however, shake off the thought that, at some point, the tide of SNP victory would stop. It didn't happen.

Stewart took his seat in a landslide result, winning a 12,000 majority over Labour and becoming the first MP to have been born in Castlemilk. As he made his victory speech, his partner Gordon and his parents watched proudly from the sidelines. Stewart's father is still a school janitor and his mum is still a school cleaner, but their son is now a Member of Parliament. 'This place is just bricks,' he says outside the House of Parliament. 'MPs set the standard on how open, connected, and accountable this place is.'

19. CHRIS STEPHENS
GLASGOW SOUTH WEST

Chris Stephens was born in Glasgow in 1973 into a working-class family. Living in council association housing in Erskine, the ideals and values of trade unionism – of fairness, equality, and unity – were ingrained into him from an early age. These values shaped the formative years of his childhood, but in the public arena Chris could barely see anyone advocating or standing up for the values that his parents had taught him to hold so dear. 'I am the third generation in terms of SNP support,' he said. Although both his grandparents and parents had been lifelong SNP voters, it wouldn't be until hearing Jim Sillars' speeches espousing trade unionist values in the 1998 by-election that he became inspired to join the SNP. Joining the SNP shortly after Sillars' by-election victory when he was just sixteen, Chris became an activist for the party at the height of protest against poll tax.

Soon after joining the SNP, Chris started a youth apprenticeship with Strathclyde regional council while also attending James Watt College to gain his qualifications in Public Administration. After securing full-time employment with Strathclyde Regional Council – then later Glasgow City Council, where he remained until he was eventually elected as MP in 2015 – Chris became heavily involved with the trade union Unison, initially becoming the Glasgow City branch's Youth Officer, before becoming the branch's treasurer and the vice chair. Initially he took on these roles because colleagues had asked him to, but he soon sought to defend fellow workers while budgets were cut and people suffered the consequences.

Over the next twenty years, Chris became a senior activist in Unison and one of the union's lead negotiators. At the same time as he became so heavily involved in his trade union, he also became involved more deeply with the SNP: 'The first election I stood in was for Glasgow city council in 1995. I was fifty-three votes short and the Labour councillor that beat me joined the SNP a year later.'

1995 was Chris's first electoral defeat but it wasn't to be his last. He became a consistent activist for the party, standing in many seats where the hope for victory was slim. Losing in these elections was never a pleasant experience, and the 2011 Scottish Parliament election defeat hit the hardest. Chris, having previously contested the constituency of Glasgow Pollok in 2007, was selected to once again face-off against Johann Lamont, the then Deputy Leader of the Scottish Labour Party. Despite a massive SNP surge across Scotland, Chris was beaten by the slim margin of 623 votes.

It was a gutting experience to come so close, but Chris quickly picked himself up because he realised that, with an SNP majority government, it meant that a Referendum on independence would become a reality. Chris became a campaign coordinator for Glasgow Pollok's Yes movement and spent the better part of three years fighting across Pollok to ensure there was a Yes vote. 'Pollok had the highest individual number of Yes votes in Glasgow,' he boasted, and it was that level of support that convinced him that the Referendum would result in a Yes vote: 'I thought we were going to win it. Our experience in Pollok and the enthusiasm we saw in the lead up to the vote was inspiring. You could see and get a sense that we were going to win the Referendum in Glasgow, and during the 2011 election it had been a similar experience. So I thought, like it had in the 2011 election, that sense of feeling we were seeing in Pollok would be replicated across the whole country.' Unfortunately this was not to be: while Glasgow voted Yes, the country as a whole would vote to remain within the United Kingdom.

In the days after the Referendum Chris took some solace, both in the fact that Glasgow had voted Yes and that across social media there had been an outpouring of support. It was the rise of the SNP's trade union group's membership – doubling to over 2,000 members in a week – which gave Chris the belief that the Referendum had fundamentally changed the SNP. His renewed resilience would only intensify when, two weeks after the Referendum on the date of the group's AGM, its membership sat at over 10,400. 'That is when I realised a sea change was coming,' he remarked.

Asked to put forward his name by members of his local branch and inspired by the surging membership of the party, the obvious next step for Chris was to stand for election. Having run against Ian Davidson in 2010, Chris was re-selected to fight the same seat of Glasgow South West: 'When you are the candidate you don't want to make any assumptions. Canvassing had us consistently in front across the board but even with so many new volunteers we were taking it all with a pinch of salt.'

As the election progressed, areas that had been Labour in 2010 and 2011 completely flipped over to the SNP. A change in the mood of the whole city could be seen on the ground: house after house plastered their windows with SNP posters, proudly proclaiming their support for the SNP. On election night, not one ballot box in the party's sampling showed that the Labour Party had beaten the SNP. As the final results were announced Chris secured a massive victory, overturning a majority of over 14,000 and securing a majority of nearly 10,000 votes for the SNP. As he celebrated with his campaign team, his defeated opponent marched over to the television cameras to call for the resignation of Jim Murphy as Leader of the Scottish Labour Party.

20. CAROL MONAGHAN
GLASGOW NORTH WEST

As a teacher for many years, Carol Monaghan 'always had great ambitions for the kids I [would] teach, I wouldn't let people put them down'. This mentality translated into her politics: 'Why shouldn't Scotland be a world player? We aren't too wee, too stupid, or too poor.' Carol was born in 1972, and grew up in Glasgow, where her parents were a teacher and gardener and money was always tight. After school, Carol went to Strathclyde University primarily because 'financially it wasn't an option to go anywhere outside of Glasgow to study'.

Carol did not get involved in student politics at university but she focused on more major issues and attended anti-poll tax demos. Indeed, at the time she felt politics was just 'people shouting at each other for the sake of it without making any progress'. She was also at university at the same time as Jim Murphy who she vividly remembers 'Standing on the steps shouting about the poll tax and organising student demos against trident, which is really interesting when you see where he is now.'

Carol graduated from Strathclyde University with a BSc (hons) in Laser Physics and Optoelectronics in 1993. She then went on to train as a teacher, gaining a PGCE in Physics and Mathematics. After achieving her PGCE Carol moved away from Glasgow for the first time to teach in Romania for a year which was an eye-opening experience: 'I was teaching English mainly but we were working with the local Roma population. They were socially excluded and had their own schools, had their own areas. So we were doing work with them, but we had so little resources that we brought drawing materials from Glasgow with us and did fun projects. I was with an organisation called World's Exchange. It was incredibly interesting, as the part of Romania I was in was Transylvania. The main population was Hungarian, but there was also a strong Romanian population there which is very segregated and the two sides don't get on, and then there are the Roma that nobody likes either.'

Upon returning to Scotland Carol went on to work in many schools around Glasgow, including fourteen years at Hyndland Secondary as Head of Physics and Head of Science. She also spent two years as a Glasgow University lecturer training future teachers. Furthermore, as an SQA consultant, Carol has been involved in developing physics qualifications at a national level.

Carol got involved in campaigning for the SNP in 2007 while heavily pregnant: 'I had always voted for the SNP, but my family had always been Labour-voting. My dad [...] had got himself out of poverty through hard work, and he always instilled the confidence to make your own decisions in his kids.' Carol discussed her move from teaching into politics, explaining that in the past she hadn't thought about entering politics: 'I didn't have any political ambitions and I was happy to be an activist and a supporter. After the Referendum seeing more and more members joining the party I knew that the political vision that had been created in the Referendum campaign was being resorted. I went to see Nicola [Sturgeon] at the Hydro, and to see those 12,000 people it really dawned on me that there were a lot of us now!'

'As the Westminster nominations started to come in, I went around trying to convince women to put themselves forward but no women wanted to stand in Glasgow North West, and people started asking me. I initially said that I couldn't because I had kids. Then I was going to Ireland for a wedding with my husband, and we were talking about candidates. It was the Saturday and the nominations closed on the

Monday and I finally decided that if we couldn't get another woman to stand then I would do it. By the time we had arrived in Ireland I had changed my mind, but my husband had already phoned and got my nomination into the party. He convinced me to keep my name in the ring.'

In her campaign for Westminster Carol said that she 'concentrated on what we were doing, and ignored the Labour campaign'. Like many of the 56, her campaign was all about giving a positive message: 'The campaign was positive and fun, and we just watched the Labour vote collapse. Every single day we were out in force.' On the election night Carol went home at nine in the evening but couldn't sleep: 'I got the phone call from my husband at 12am saying [that] it was looking good and that I should get ready to come in, but then I got a call from my election agent saying that it was too close to call. So then I was panicking, but he was just being a git! I went in and saw the piles for us and we knew at that point that I had won and won well.'

Carol paid tribute to her inspirations in politics: 'Alex Salmond has influenced me as a great orator. However, it was Nicola Sturgeon that pushed me to do this and her promotion of women in politics.' When asked what she wants to achieve in her position in Westminster Carol answered: 'What drives me is getting more powers for Scotland. We need the power in Scotland to make our own decisions. We are now seeing the effects of these really savage cuts and there has got to be a better way. There needs to be a level playing field for everybody and that can't happen in austerity.' Carol's parting words stressed the need for Scotland's voice to be heard: 'I really want Scotland to have a coherent voice. We will fight austerity, because it is creating a society that is removing opportunity and creating more and more barriers to young people's life chances. We need to be taking the hurdles down, not putting them in people's way.'

21. NATALIE MCGARRY
GLASGOW EAST

'The chants of 'Maggie, Maggie, Maggie! Out! Out! Out!' was the soundtrack to my childhood,' joked the new MP for Glasgow East, Natalie McGarry. Born in Dunfermline but raised in Inverkeithing, Natalie's parents were both passionate protestors against the actions and policies of the Thatcher and Major governments. From as early an age as three, Natalie attended many protests with her parents, and the family fed the miners during the general strikes of the mid-eighties. 'I remember going to anti-poll [tax] and anti-nuclear rallies [...] and when people were going to Butlins, we were off protesting in Glasgow or Calton Hill.' It was no ordinary childhood, but it was perfect for Natalie who loved the atmosphere of the protests. Her mother was elected to Fife council in 1986 and, as one of the tiny number of councillors in opposition to the Labour Party, politics were at her very core.

This passion for politics translated from mother to daughter easily. Rather than being something that Natalie was taken to, protests became something she attended willingly; the early eighties and nineties formed Natalie's politics, at the same time that the SNP were becoming a centre-left wing force in Scotland. It wasn't the SNP's ideology that originally attracted Natalie to the party: it was the strong and powerful female voices that she saw within it. Winnie Ewing had at this time become an SNP MEP and had the nickname of 'Madame Ecosse'. Although this was originally intended as an insult, it became a badge of honour for Ewing. Natalie was told stories of Ewing, and saw her as an inspiration: 'There was a flamboyance and mysticism about her,' Natalie recalled. There were not many women in positions of power, but the figures of Ewing and her own mother inspired Natalie to join the party.

While Natalie's politics were different to the Labour Party, growing up on the same street as the office of Gordon Brown meant the Labour Party was hard to avoid. It was the former Labour MEP, Alex Falconer, with whom she had the most interactions: 'Alex was a character,' she remarked. 'I used to pass his office in the morning to get the school bus. And he'd come out his office and try to pin badges on me. I soon learned not to take the Labour ones, and he moved along and gave me trade union ones.'

After high school Natalie was accepted to study both Law and Politics at the University of Edinburgh. It was short-lived, however, because Natalie dropped out of university after her first year. Full of predominantly upper- and middle-class students, The University of Edinburgh didn't feel the right environment for her. On informing her university Director of Studies of her decision to leave, a tense discussion occurred: 'When I spoke to my Director of Studies he accused me of trying to get into Edinburgh Law School by the back door. Which was funny because I actually had the grades to get in by the front door.' Yet a university degree was, however, still what she wanted to achieve, so Natalie applied to study Law at the University of Aberdeen instead, hoping that escaping the capital would provide a different experience.

Moving to Aberdeen proved to be the right decision, and after four years Natalie graduated with a Bachelor's degree in Law but she didn't want to actually join the legal profession: 'I had perhaps been inspired by Ally McBeal in the courtroom and then realised that the Law is nothing like it. [...] I realised I was more interested in the process of things and researching where laws come from. I was especially interested in Roman Law and how these principles had been carried forward into Scots Law, but I realised living in the past in that aspect was not particularly a good idea for future practice as a Solicitor.' Instead she chose to return home to Inverkeithing, where she continued working in McDonald's – she had worked for the company throughout university – and spent time thinking about exactly what she wanted to do in the future.

Eventually Natalie moved away from Fife to seek work in the charity sector. While she had always felt passionate about politics, the idea of electoral politics didn't feel right for her either. The political ideas that she held dear – of solving injustice, bringing an end to poverty, and supporting real equality – were still important, and Natalie believed that by working in the charity sector she could help to solve at least some of these problems for a small amount of people. Her first job was helping to support unemployed parents in Cambuslang, yet the charity never seemed able to stem the tide of people who required help and it didn't have enough money to support all those that needed it. This insight prompted Natalie to move into the third sector to work with organisations across the country, to secure funding that would enable them to carry out work supporting the most vulnerable in society.

When the idea of an independence referendum became a reality following the 2011 Scottish elections, Natalie felt that she couldn't stand on the sidelines any longer. She became one of the co-founders of the influential group Women for Independence with former SSP MSP Carolyn Leckie; she joked that the group was 'created over a glass of wine'. The group garnered support from across all of Scotland's political parties and became the catalyst for many other Yes Groups to develop across the country. Working on the Women for Independence campaign also led to heavy involvement with the SNP, around the time of the SNP's vote over NATO membership. As Natalie's childhood had been spent protesting against nuclear weapons, at the vote at the SNP's conference in October 2012 she spoke in defence of the SNP's then-current policy on NATO membership: 'It was the first time I had spoken in public since I was sixteen and I felt really strongly about it [...] I was gutted at the result, but that is something you have to learn. How to lose.'

The NATO vote didn't stop Natalie from continuing to get more involved with both the SNP and the Referendum campaign. In many ways, she believes that speaking at the NATO vote enabled her to find her voice during the Referendum. Following that debate Natalie became the de-facto spokeswoman for Women for Independence and found herself selected as the SNP's candidate in the 2014 Cowdenbeath by-election. However standing in the seat wasn't easy. Firstly, many initially thought that Natalie's mum was standing when they saw the name Natalie McGarry on the ballot, and secondly, Natalie had to run against the well-known Leader of Fife Council and the future Scottish Labour Deputy, Alex Rowley. Although unsurprisingly defeated, Natalie gained experience of running in an election, which proved very useful less than a year later.

After the defeat in the Referendum Natalie was selected as the SNP's candidate for Glasgow East, going up against the Shadow Secretary of State for Scotland, Margaret Curran. The Labour Party made a gargantuan effort to keep the seat: they made many policy announcements and there were multiple visits from both the party's UK Leader Ed Miliband and Scottish Leader Jim Murphy to show support. Despite these efforts, poll after poll suggested that the SNP were on course to secure a major victory: 'The Labour Party were throwing everything and the kitchen sink at Glasgow East,' Natalie recalled. 'What that demonstrated was the complete lack of awareness on the Labour Party's part about what people in the constituency were telling them.' On election night the SNP and Natalie won the seat of Glasgow East with over a 30% swing towards the party.

After the election, although over one third of the new MPs in Parliament were female, this wasn't enough for Natalie: having grown up fiercely opposed to the actions of Margaret Thatcher – who she described as 'rising to the top of high office and then pulling up the ladder behind her' – she has sworn to never follow the same path. 'I stand here on the shoulders of many women,' Natalie said during her maiden speech to the Parliament. 'I am held up, too, by the thousands of women who rose up in the Referendum. Women for Independence enabled me to find my voice. Now that I have found it, I will never tire. I am but one woman, but make no mistake, there are many, many like me.'

22. MARGARET FERRIER
RUTHERGLEN AND HAMILTON WEST

Margaret Ferrier was born in 1961 on the south side of Glasgow. She moved to King's Park when she was five and her childhood was an experience typical for Glasgow in the sixties: de-industrialisation and decline had caused rampant poverty, and while her family was always able to get by, living pay-cheque-to-pay-cheque was stressful. As the youngest sibling of three, she was shielded from much of the hardship as her parents, brother, and sister worked. But as she grew up, more and more responsibility was placed on her shoulders as she explained: 'My father was very ill and passed away when I was nineteen so I had to go straight into work, because it was just my mum and I.'

When Margaret left high school she got a job working in retail with Goldbergs in Glasgow. The city also managed to pull itself out of the slump that de-industrialisation had caused, and more and more opportunities became available in newer, service-based businesses. Margaret moved from retail into the growing service sector to work for British Telecom, but the memory of the industrial industry's collapse in the city still loomed over her and her family: both her siblings became involved in their trade unions, and the ideals of the Red Clydesiders were never far from discussion. 'You were raised Labour,' she said.

Margaret's politics developed via a different strand to that of her siblings: 'I got involved with Amnesty International. I liked the idea of making sure there was no injustice done.' For Margaret, the plight of political prisoners became a serious issue, and she spent her time writing to foreign countries and leaders asking for political prisoners to be freed. Amnesty International was Margaret's route into politics, but it was politics with a small 'p'.

Eventually, Margaret moved her career into the courier industry, working her way up from customer services to the operations control room: 'It was exciting, the buzz of trying to get parcels out the door and delivered in time. I just enjoyed it.' Along with her career, her own politics started to develop and she decided to join the Labour Party. She joined the Labour Party's Pollok branch at the same time as the future Labour leader Johann Lamont and her husband were running for the Scottish Parliament and Council. She never felt truly comfortable within the party: 'Meetings were really boring and mostly full of men, there was no gender balance. All I did for them was deliver leaflets.' Completely unenthused, she left in the early 2000s and became a floating voter. Despite the establishment of the Scottish Parliament politics had no hold over her, and it wasn't until 2007 – upon hearing the arguments of Alex Salmond – that she started to become engaged again. 'I think at the start I didn't want to believe I was being persuaded because I was always brought up to be a Labour voter. A lot of what he was saying made sense to me. Eventually, as I started to listen more, I found that a lot of it really resonated with me.' Like many in Scotland, Margaret had begun to change her mind about the SNP and the Labour Party: the Iraq War and the Blair government conflicted with Margaret's values, and slowly the SNP began to fill the space that Labour had vacated.

The turning point for Margaret came in May 2011. Alex Salmond had just completed the final debate of the Scottish Elections in the Perth Concert Hall for the BBC, and the crowd was roaring behind him. Margaret – until this point a Labour voter – was in the audience and she spoke to Alex Salmond. It then became clear to her that the SNP was her political home, and to the then-First Minister she simply said: 'I'm a traditional Labour person and I've been voting Labour, but tonight it all just sat right with me.'

A month later she joined the party. Explaining her decision to covert to the SNP, Margaret states 'The Labour Party left me, it wasn't the other way around.' From the first day of joining the party, Margaret threw herself into campaigning. Unlike her experience of the Labour party all those years before, she found enthusiasm with the SNP: 'I had immersed myself completely. I was at every by-election I could get to, I wanted to be very active in the party.' Margaret crossed the country campaigning for the SNP, reigniting a passion for politics that she hadn't felt since she was a teenager writing letters to Amnesty International.

The referendum campaign then took over her life in many ways. Acting as an Organiser for Yes Rutherglen, Margaret spent weekends campaigning, while weekday evenings were spent canvassing neighbourhoods: all her spare time was channelled into the campaign for a Yes vote. Yet South Lanarkshire, like many other parts of Scotland, voted No in the Referendum. Devastated by the result, Margaret shrugged off any thought of running for election in 2015: campaigning for Margaret was about ideals – about fighting injustice – and not about being elected. But after receiving support from councillors and party members, she decided to put herself forward to see what running in a national election would be like.

Canvass results and national polls quickly began to suggest that she wasn't just running in a national election; it looked like she might actually win her seat. Her opponent was the young Shadow Minister for Energy Tom Greatrex, who had worked for the Labour Party since the days of Donald Dewar. Margaret had only stood in one previous election – a council by-election in 2013 which she had lost – but everything seemed to point to victory: 'The canvassing results we were getting were sensational,' she said. Indeed, this was replicated on election night when Margaret took the seat of a 31.1% swing from the Labour Party.

Margaret's political journey embodies the change that Scottish politics has undergone in her lifetime: born on the banks of the Clyde shipyards, and having witnessed the speeches of Jimmy Reid, she was the traditional Labour voter. Yet although she was raised to support Labour, she now stands as an SNP Member of Parliament. In her

Maiden speech to the Commons Margaret said, 'Why were we elected? Because we listened to the people of our nation and we will continue to listen to them.'

23. MARTIN DOCHERTY
WEST DUNBARTONSHIRE

Martin Docherty started life in Faifley, Clydebank, where his childhood home was on the ground floor of a 1950s tenement. His family then relocated to Dalmuir, where the family were lucky to get a house with a front and a back door, as Martin explained: 'We were overcrowded, and I also had a younger brother who was profoundly mentally and physically disabled, so it was one of the few houses where we were able to get a ramp put in for wheelchair access and help things for the family.' Martin attended St Joseph's Primary School then St Stephen's in Dalmuir, before attending high school at St Columba.

Leaving school with no formal qualifications, Martin found employment in the Singer sewing machine factory. After the closure of the factory Martin moved jobs: 'I was working in a sweetie factory and I put on my CV that I was a 'confectioner'. The reality was that I would stir pots of fondant and desiccated coconut to make macaroon bars. It certainly wasn't artisan, that's for sure. So that was my first working job.' Martin then went into seminary study for priesthood, which he eventually left. Returning home to Clydebank, Martin secured a job in catering and joined the Scottish National Party in 1991, before becoming the youngest councillor in the country in 1992 for the old

Clydebank district council. Martin worked for the council for around five years before returning to education in 1997 to undertake an HND in Business and Tourism. From there, Martin moved to Essex University: 'I eventually got into the Department of Government and graduated in 2000 with a degree in Politics from one of the great departments of Government in Europe, and I was honoured as I was the first member of my family to attend university.' After gaining his degree Martin studied for a Master's at the Glasgow School of Art where he researched 'the relationship between the construction of the Scottish parliament and democracy. Needless to say, no one wanted to grant me an interview because there was a public enquiry at the time so my research was quite difficult.'

Politics were always a big part of Martin's life: 'My dad is a coppersmith to trade, he worked in what was John Brown's shipyard and then John Brown's engineering and he was extremely involved in the upper Clyde shipyard strikes and he was actually a shop steward. Our family life was always quite political and he was very much involved in the Labour movement, I have to say, not the Labour party. I remember our councillor at the time was Jimmy Reed, and he was a communist, so there was always that left-wing Labour movement in politics and, for me, my natural inclination when I first voted in the European elections was to vote SNP. It was a party that spoke to me about certain areas of social justice and the idea that government should be as local as possible. In terms of my identity, I never felt an affinity with the UK [...] so my natural inclination was to join the SNP and I did so when I was twenty-one.'

Martin further explained: 'The miners' strikes were a big influence on me. Coming from Clydebank, one of the biggest issues has always been nuclear arms and, as a young child I was always mindful of the horror of war in Clydebank and the Clydebank Blitz, one of the worst elements of the Blitzkriegs of 1941, and, per head of population, we probably suffered more than anywhere else in the British Isles. So, the impact of war was a huge influence on my political background and from going on many CND marches from a very young age. My sister was very instrumental in forcing me at that time to take recognition of nuclear power and nuclear energy and nuclear weapons being so close to us in Clydebank and across West Dunbartonshire, so I would say that the CND was the most critical element that got me involved in politics and [it] also really did focus me on the SNP.'

The result of the Referendum was a double-edged sword for Martin: 'I was campaigning in Glasgow [...] so I was absolutely delighted that Glasgow voted Yes and the bittersweetness of it is that my own home, Clydebank, Dumbarton, and the Vale [of Leven], also voted Yes. I still have hope that my term in this parliament will hopefully be short, however short that may be, and it will be part of a process leading to an independent sovereign Scotland.'

Martin went on to talk about his election campaign: 'The campaign was great, we've got over 1600 SNP members from the Yoker Mill Road to the shores of the Inchmurrin, across Clydebank, Dumbarton and the Vale of Leven, and they made that campaign a great campaign. It was hard-fought but some of the returns we were getting by Christmas time we chose not to believe so we could remain focused on the job ahead.'

In the 2015 May election Martin won the West Dunbartonshire seat with 59% of the vote: 'My family are absolutely delighted that I've become an MP, my partner John is absolutely overjoyed, we're still a wee bit in shock and trying to take it all in, so is my dad – he never thought in a month of Sundays that I would be sitting in here speaking to you about a book about 56 MPs who all happen to be SNP members! So the family, my sister and my brother, are all absolutely delighted.'

Martin then spoke about what drives him as a politician: 'One of the most critical things are nuclear weapons and that links to equality, because that's a political choice and it's a choice about whether we invest in the apocalypse, to be blunt – we can call it weapons of mass destruction but it's the end of life as we know it – or we choose to invest in a future which ends a low-wage economy, which invests in a national health service which we believe can do a lot more but we need the resources to do that, and which children from my background, from Clydebank, Dumbarton and the Vale of Leven, have a sustainable future. I hear much in the chamber about inspiring people and aspiration; well, my aspiration is to have access to a decent day's wage for a decent job and jobs which can be created in West Dunbartonshire, which allow people to remain in their communities. To me, the answer to that is independence and that can only be delivered through the Scottish National Party.'

Asked about the main influences on his life, Martin answered: 'The people in politics who have inspired me are my father, my late mother whose politics were about family life and how that can have a profound impact on the way you live your life, my aunts and uncles and the way in which they conducted themselves in terms of their political debates – we would always have big political debates throughout the year at family occasions – and whether we disagreed or not. My sister was a huge influence in terms of the campaign against nuclear disarmament and my partner John has a huge influence in reminding me that we need to understand our communities better by being more representative of them, not just reflecting what they need but actually making changes which meet their needs. They're the kind of people who inspire me. If you were to ask if there was a politician who inspires me there's probably three people: a guy called Harvey Milk who is a member of the LGBT community who was the first openly gay politician to be elected in the United States and [he] died for it. There's then a guy called Elijah Harper who brought down the Meech Lake Accord in Canada because it excluded the native Canadian population and he is a frail, fragile human being with an alcohol problem – he's no political hero – but he's an inspiration for what he did with his community. The there's Rosa Parks who took a seat and changed the world.'

Martin's vision of a future Scotland is 'a place where there is justice, social justice, where we're all equal – not just before the law but before each other – in a society where we aspire to be the best we can be for our community, where we recognise that we can pay into a system because we want to work, not for what we can get out of it, where we have an NHS which, thankfully through our Scottish government, is maintained as a public service, a Scotland that's independent and sovereign, and where the people are sovereign. Not a parliament, not an individual, but the people of Scotland, as we make sure that the community of Scotland regains its independence.'

24. MHAIRI BLACK
PAISLEY AND RENFREWSHIRE SOUTH

'You know,' said Mhairi Black, contemplating the absurdity of sitting in the centre of Portcullis House, 'I'm just starting to realise that I am quite bizarre [as a young MP in Westminster], but also that I'm quite lucky.' Whether bizarre occurrence or sheer luck, Mhairi is now the youngest MP in the House of Commons since 1832. Born in Glasgow's Southern General, Mhairi was raised in the outskirts of Paisley: 'I look back in retrospect and realise we grew up watching it all decline,' she says. 'We grew up watching the town centre become emptier, and more and more pubs, shops, and restaurants shutting. It is the same story for too many communities in Scotland.'

While growing up, the idea of going to university really motivated Mhairi. Her two parents had come from backgrounds of poverty and Mhairi had been told stories of how hard they had worked to get to university: 'I thought [that] if I am clever enough I want to take advantage of it. My mum grew up with nothing, and my Dad was very similar. They worked their backsides off to get to university, so, I thought, I need to do the same here.'

Mhairi struggled with high school, finding the whole experience restrictive. When she left at the age of sixteen – a plan she had had for a while – she still was absolutely determined to go to university. Although she didn't want to let herself or her parents down, during the year that she prepared to apply for university, the Coalition Government's new tuition fee rise kicked in for English Universities. In response, Scottish universities started upping their grade requirements 'to balance things out because so many people were trying to come to Scotland', meaning that Mhairi had to achieve top grades to have any hope of getting into the University of Glasgow.

In the end she narrowly missed out a conditional offer: 'I was gutted, but I thought I am not giving up.' Mhairi managed to secure entry into the University of Glasgow's summer school and upped her grades to gain entry for a BA in Music and Politics. Music proved to be too theoretical and not practical enough for Mhairi to remain interested, so after one year she dropped the course and focused on Politics.

Mhairi's political training wasn't really in the classroom, however, but out on the streets and at doors during the Referendum. As an ardent supporter of independence, Mhairi had been first spotted by the SNP's former Deputy Leader Jim Sillars, at a speaking event in Paisley. They shared a podium for Yes Paisley and Sillars, so impressed by Mhairi's performance, invited her out to campaign with him: 'He pulled me aside and said, "give me your email address". He wanted me along for the day to see how old-style campaigning was done.' The campaigning event turned out to be the launch of Sillar's 'Margo Mobile' campaign, and Sillars later asked her to join him for the rest of the Referendum campaign. Meant to be an initial learning experience for Mhairi, it did in fact turn into a full campaign schedule across Scotland and throughout the Referendum; when she wasn't campaigning alongside her dad in Paisley, she was with Sillars and the Margo Mobile. It is likely that this part of the campaign set in motion everything that was to follow, because soon Mhairi became a star campaigner and well-known face throughout the local SNP groups.

The Referendum for Mhairi ended in a bitter defeat both nationally and locally: 'We were all dejected,' she declared. Despite the fact that all the SNP's work undertaken throughout the entire campaign had led to defeat, Mhairi refused to remain depressed: 'I thought we had fought too hard for this and I am not going back in my box. What amazed and heartened me was I was not the only person feeling that way – it became very clear very quickly, with the surge in membership of the SNP, that something was changing.'

Despite the encouragement of many of her fellow SNP members, it was never in her mind to stand for election. It was through speaking with Jim Sillars and Ian Lawson that she considered to stand, as Mhari explained: 'Ian made a good point saying, "what was wrong with being twenty?"'. There are certain conventions that you just take for granted and you just accept them, but sometimes it takes someone to challenge them before you rethink. Shouldn't parliament represent everybody? You're old enough to go to war, old enough to pay taxes but not old enough to vote in the chamber on what those taxes should be spent on? That doesn't weigh up.'

Eventually Mhairi was convinced and she put her name forward for the party's selection. In truth, however, she didn't expect to receive the nomination, and on the day she was due to find out if she was successful in the party's selection she did what she did every Wednesday: volunteer for her local Oxfam shop. Unknown to Mhairi – who was working in the basement of Oxform where nobody was able to contact her for hours – the party's Campaign Director Angus Robertson had tweeted the winners of the selection. While Twitter was buzzing with talk about her candidacy, she was sorting out books in the basement of Oxfam. When she finally surfaced much later that day her mobile exploded with calls, tweets, and messages about her selection. A phone call with her dad confirmed that she would be going up against Labour's Shadow Foreign Secretary, Douglas Alexander, at the General Election.

Mhairi's father acted as her election agent and coordinated Mhairi's campaign, and his campaigning activities were nothing that she wasn't accustomed to. Mhairi had cut her political teeth alongside him, as she explained: 'My dad and I were like a team canvassing during the Referendum,' she explained. He had been her rock throughout the Referendum and also in her selection to fight the seat. Memories of the Referendum filled Mhairi with dread on Election day: 'Our canvassing was phenomenal, but I remembered the canvassing during the Referendum – it was phenomenal too – and we lost,' she reflected. Yet on this occasion things seemed different, not just for her but for her fellow fifty-eight candidates around Scotland, and on the day she felt an aura of confidence: 'We went to a scheme in Johnstone called the Highway Road,' she remarked. 'It was one of the hardest Labour areas within our constituency, but when we went canvassing I didn't meet a single Labour voter. Door after door was just filled with angry ex-Labour voters happy to see us.' She relished the campaigning aspects of elections, as a young SNP activist on her campaign observed: 'Confident in her ideals and convictions, [Mhairi] portrayed something to her electorate that people just weren't used to. She was able to convince people she really believed what she was saying.'

At the close of polls Mhairi ventured to the Lagoon Leisure Centre in Paisley to hear her constituency's verdict, both on herself and the SNP. The Leisure Centre was not a place of happy memories: only eight months previously, in the very same hall, she had watched the returning officer declare that Renfrewshire had voted No in the Referendum. Yet in the General Election, as SNP supporters sampled box after box of votes, it became clear to everyone that she would win the seat. Taking to the stage wearing the grey suit that her friends had so long teased her about, she carried two specific things: one was her victory speech and the other was the scarf that belonged to her political hero Margo MacDonald. 'She [MacDonald] was everything anybody could hope to be, she never put a foot wrong. She was an exemplary person, never mind politician.' Clutching the scarf that Margo's husband Jim Sillars had given to Mhairi during the campaign, her face broke into a smile and she gave a nod to her raving supporters while the same returning officer from the Referendum announced the results. Overturning Douglas Alexander's 16,000 majority in Paisley and Renfrewshire South by gaining a 5,864 majority, Mhairi ended the Scottish Labour Party's seventy-year-long electoral dominance of the constituency.

Mhairi defeated the Scottish Labour party in its heartlands, but in many ways she saw her victory as a triumph of the traditional socialist values that she believed that the Labour Party used to embody. In her maiden speech to the House of Commons, which has been viewed over 10 million times to date, Mhairi drew inspiration from one of the last Labour Party MPs to hold true to that socialist political platform:

'Tony Benn once said that in politics there are weathercocks and sign posts. Weathercocks will spin in whatever direction the wind of public opinion may blow them, no matter what principle they may have to compromise. And then there are signposts, signposts which stand true, and tall, and principled. And they point in the direction and they say this is the way to a better society and it is my job to convince you why Tony Benn was right when he said the only people worth remembering in politics were signposts.'

25. GAVIN NEWLANDS
PAISLEY AND RENFREWSHIRE NORTH

Gavin Newlands was born in 1980 in Paisley's new town, before the family moved to Renfrew in 1984. At school in Renfrew Gavin often suffered because of his shy nature: 'I didn't have a great deal of confidence in myself when I was growing up,' he said. While he proved to be a smart and well-liked student he felt out of place, but Gavin's shyness in school was in complete contrast to his nature at home. Gavin's Dad was an ardent supporter of the SNP, and he often attended SNP campaigning events to support the party's candidate while leafleting or cheering from atop a bus. When it came to the SNP it was very much 'like father, like son': Gavin's interest in the SNP was so great that he joined the party's youth wing in its anti-poll tax activities alongside his father when he was only twelve years old.

Despite his interest in politics, it was not what he wanted to do with his life. Instead Gavin aspired to become a journalist and after finishing high school he attended James Watt College, hoping to boost his qualifications to move into a journalism course at university. It was, however, during his time at college that he had a job at McDonalds in Glasgow Airport, and as the company offered more and more opportunities for advancement, Gavin was forced to choose between his stable job or continuing with his journalistic ambitions: 'It was quite a big decision for me, because I really had wanted to go on to become a journalist. But when the offer of a salaried position was there it was hard to turn down.' In the end he decided to take up the position in management, convincing himself that securing a stable job with a good income was the right decision. However, with hindsight, another major figure had played a huge part in deciding his future that, at the time, he hadn't realised: 'Looking back, one of the main reasons that I took the job was that Lynn [his future wife] had just started working there, so thinking about it now, I don't regret it for a second. I've now got a wonderful wife, and two beautiful daughters. So really I couldn't ask for much else.'

While the dream of university and journalism motivated Gavin, he still retained an avid interest in politics and in supporting the SNP. In 2011, alongside the election of an SNP majority government, he started to become heavily involved in the Referendum campaign in Renfrew. Despite all the work he and his fellow campaigners put into the Referendum campaign, on polling day Gavin was convinced that the result wouldn't be a Yes: 'I think I can be a bit pessimistic. I remember going to the Referendum count thinking that we would lose 43/57. It was 45/55, but it didn't make it feel much better.'

After the Referendum was over things started to go back to normal for Gavin. Standing for election wasn't on the cards and he knew that, whichever candidate was nominated, he would support them at the General Election. There was, however, a small consideration in the back of his mind that maybe this was the right time for him to run for election: 'My wife in the end convinced me to do it. She said that if I wanted it then I should just go for it. So I put my name forward but hadn't actually expected to get selected.'

Despite his pessimism Gavin was selected as the SNP's candidate for Paisley and Renfrewshire North, having gone up against a man that had been the area's MP for over a decade and who, at the last election, secured more than 50% of the vote when the SNP couldn't get above 20%: 'I knew it was going to be a tough challenge. But we would have a much bigger chance of winning than any SNP candidate had ever had before.' Deciding that in order to win the election the party would need a full-time candidate, Gavin left his management job with McDonalds in February and spent every day of the next four months campaigning across the entire constituency.

'There were so many places that, as the SNP, we hadn't ever door-knocked before. We'd always done tele-canvassing, but I was determined that we would try to knock every door in the constituency.' By the end of the campaign tens of thousands of doors had been knocked on and canvassed by SNP campaigners, and all the results indicated that it would be a victory for the SNP. Yet Gavin couldn't be convinced: 'I kept speaking to people who would say to me that they now saw the SNP as the natural home of the working-class vote [...] but again the pessimist in me said that we might not have done enough.'

On polling day Gavin made it clear that he did not want to have any forewarning of the result or hear about how good or bad the ballot box sampling was on the night. Undertaking three canvassing sessions a day every day, the final two weeks of the campaign had been non-stop for him, and although he had maintained that knocking on those extra doors would help, by the close of polls he thought that the Labour Party might well hold onto the seat. After ten o'clock came he was terrified at the prospect of the result and other things started going through his mind: 'I kept thinking that if I lost it would be down to the job centre [on] Friday morning, no matter how tired I was.' Both his wife and friends tried to convince him to be more confident, but all he wanted to do was see the final result.

The thought of having to go back to the same place that had delivered the heart-wrenching Referendum result continued to weigh on Gavin, but finally he got a call from his election agent at 22:40pm telling him to get his victory speech ready. The call allowed Gavin to breathe a sigh of relief and when he finally got to the count he was met with a sea of smiling activists, all waiting to see the result they were sure was going to be announced. It was an amazing result for the SNP, with the party winning just over 50% of the vote and securing a 26.5% swing from Labour. It was a night that Gavin had dreamed of but hadn't dared to think it could become a reality. 'The vision I put forward is that I want to make the lives of my constituents easier,' he said later about the campaign. 'Whether that is through the power of argument, protecting them from Tory cuts, or helping them through the office of being an MP, I want to do whatever it take to make their lives easier.'

26. RONNIE COWAN
INVERCLYDE

Ronnie Cowan was born in Greenock. He grew up there, he was educated there, and he is now, quite appropriately, the MP for Greenock and the Inverclyde area. Ronnie attended Greenock Academy and 'was not their best scholar – I will say that before anybody else does!' He left school at the age of seventeen with a desire to work in IT; Ronnie secured a position as a trainee computer operator and worked his way through different ranks for thirty-five years, before running his own company in the last two years. Ronnie can still pin-point the moment he left his long career in IT to go into politics: 'It was four in the morning on the eighth of May – I remember thinking "well, that's my life in politics done and dusted". Then I went back to work after the Referendum, and for the first time in thirty-five years I thought "my heart's not in this".'

Ronnie first became interested in politics watching the TV as a child: 'I clearly remember watching the American civil rights movement – Martin Luther King, the great speeches – realising that this was something big and something important. That must have been 1959 so the early sixties when I went through that. I remember being told about the assassination of John F Kennedy when I was very young [...]

My mum told me that bad men had killed the president of the United States, which startled me. My older brother was particularly involved with getting me interested in politics – we shared a bedroom and my bedroom wall when I was eight had pictures of Che Guevara on it, though I thought he was one of the Beatles!'

'In 1971 we had a mock election in my primary school and I stood for the SNP. I have no idea why or what put me there [...] To be honest when I was eleven years of age it would've been more about flags and sport and the 'we're Scottish' type thing that put me there but I joined the party when I was sixteen. I drifted away from the party as a member in my late teens and then rejoined ten years ago. I was finally at a stage in my life where I could go to meetings, get involved in the fundraising, and be a voice in it. Most meetings I went to I didn't say much at all, and I wasn't the kind of person to kick down a door saying 'I am here, listen to me'. It was three or four years of sitting listening to people before I got involved beyond leafleting and that sort of thing.'

Ronnie is the son of the goalkeeper Jimmy Cowan who played for Morton and Scotland. Ronnie explained that he also has an interest in sport: 'I've played football and rugby, I've run marathons. My days of playing rugby are long over now, but there is an option to join the parliamentary rugby team – my heart's saying that I'm interested but my head is screaming don't do that as you'll break something again.' Ronnie's other passion is art: 'I like my art, I used to do some painting and drawing – I never had any talent to do anything off the back of it, but I've always enjoyed them. I'm often to be found in art galleries and buying a couple of bits of art that I've saved up for over the years.'

Ronnie was instrumental in the success of the Yes campaign in the Inverclyde area, which lost to the No side by only 86 votes, despite being a former unionist stronghold. Ronnie paid for the first run of leaflets himself and coordinated the campaign in the area. Describing the process that led from the SNP's loss in the Referendum though to him standing for election, he said: 'After the vote came in I made sure that the team that were at the count were all taken care of, that everyone got a lift home because there was tears all over the place. Sally McNair from the BBC came walking towards me with a TV crew behind her and I turned my heels and walked away because the BBC hadn't come near me in the previous two years. Someone from the *Telegraph* then came to interview me and he put a microphone down on the table to talk to me. All I wanted to tell him was that my team could look themselves in the mirror every day for the rest of their lives and know that they had done everything that they possibly could – that took about ten minutes for me to blurt out as I had big tears rolling on to his microphone because, at that point, I just lost the plot completely. I spent four days in bed afterwards, which my son likes to remind me on a regular basis, and he says when it comes to SNP campaigns of "Look dad, if you lose this is it going to be as bad as the Referendum result?".

I was down and beaten until the membership of the SNP picked up and grew. That's what got me revitalised – something was happening – something important. So I went through the vetting process which I'd been through to be a councillor beforehand, but [I had] never stood for the council. I wanted to see what the process was like. The vetting was on the same day that Nicola Sturgeon was doing her thing at the Hydro. I met Kirstin Oswald and Callum Cairn, so we all came to that together and then after I met a couple of pals and went to the Hydro [...] and I thought 'I want some of this. This is really vibrant and energetic and the way things are going to go forward.' So I chucked my hat in to be a candidate for the local SNP.'

Ronnie then went on to talk about his time in Westminster so far: 'When I'm down there I've heard a few people say they aren't used to hearing so many Scottish voices. I guess the last lot weren't perceived as being Scottish then? I've found myself in the select committee for public administration and constitution and we're looking at the EU Referendum just now and we're pulling in Lord Haywood and Jack Straw to talk to us about referendums in general, so I never avoid the opportunities to ask the questions about why they were biased or why they used the BBC and why they used the machine of government to be pro the No campaign. Every time anyone mentions the Referendum in Scotland, all the committee members turn and look at me – so apparently to them I'm now the walking, talking, expert on the Referendum. The 56 is not just a number, we also get money through the short money [system] and we use it to hire researchers and staff members so we will become a better political party because of this. We also get better offices. We got the Lib Dems whip office, which is right across the road from Parliament. We're on seven select committees and we chair two select committees, so these numbers all translate into this extra shift of power. If we use that power wisely in the next five years then the influence down there will be substantial. We can't be making too many enemies in Westminster, standing up and shouting abuse back and forth. We sit on all-parliamentary groups and select committees that have Tories on them. We do need to earn their respect to a certain extent, and we are doing that. They see us as a serious political force and not some tartan-clad, flag-waving, face-painting, nationalistic mob.'

Now he has become an MP, one of Ronnie's main focuses within his constituency is to create jobs there: 'What we have in Inverclyde is a river – lots of constituencies cannot say that. We have an opportunity [...] right by our doorstep, which we should use properly. I think that if companies can be encouraged to do, here, what they are wanting to do, [then] we can breathe life into the places along the Clyde.'

Ronnie's long-term vision for Scotland consists of broad improvements: 'We do a lot of growing up. We become independent, we become modern, outward-looking. We become an equal country and look at models around the world and see what works for us. I want Scotland to be inclusive to all, and [it] is respected and has earned respect throughout this planet.'

27. ALAN BROWN
KILMARNOCK AND LOUDOUN

Alan Brown was born in 1970 in Kilmarnock and grew up in the small burgh of Newmilns, which is approximately seven miles outside of the town. He attended the local primary school and then went on to Loudoun Academy, and he has remained in the area his entire life: Alan now lives in Galston with his wife Cyndi and their two sons. After school, Alan attended Glasgow University where he studied towards an honours degree in Civil Engineering. After graduating his first job was in the water industry, where he remained working in some capacity right up until his election in 2015. He worked as a design engineer and then project manager in the public sector for Strathclyde Regional Council for Scottish Water from 1993 until 2007. He then changed to work for a consultant engineering company Grontmij, where he worked as a principal engineer until May 2015.

Like so many of the 56, Alan developed an interest in politics at secondary school. He remembers sitting up for most of the night for the 1987 General Election – at the age of sixteen – watching the results come in despite having school the next morning. Alan's parents were never overtly political but they were SNP voters, and despite the lack of debate in his household, his 'logic from the outset' was that Scotland should be able to make its own decisions because 'the then-Tory Governments were an indication that [...] we couldn't make things any worse with independence and had an opportunity to make things significantly better.'

Alan described how he was influenced to actually participate in politics by a neighbour who was elected as a local councillor for the SNP: 'He encouraged me to be more active and put my name in for selection as an SNP councillor, which I did for the 2007 election. That in itself was a massive change in direction.' Alan's political career began when, much like his former next-door-neighbour, he was elected as an SNP councillor in the East Ayrshire Council election, 2007, for the Irvine Valley ward. He was re-elected in 2012. Over his time at the council Alan was a senior figure in the SNP delegation and held positions that included spokesperson for Planning and chair of the Grants Committee.

While a councillor, Alan got heavily involved in the Yes campaign: 'the Referendum campaign was a mix of highs and lows. I felt it was a long time before people were really engaged'. Alan particularly enjoyed meeting the new, enthusiastic, and politically engaged voters: 'It was all-consuming though, which meant I couldn't really talk about any other subject matter, which I'm sure was annoying to some work colleagues and friends. However, [I] always wanted to demonstrate the positives that independence could bring.' Like many others, in the last couple of weeks Alan was positive that Yes was going to win the Referendum. He remembered his experience of the day: 'On the day itself, I felt this great optimism but, as the day went on, I became more nervous, noting how many voters weren't looking you in the eye at the polling places. Obviously the final outcome was a gut-wrenching disappointment and the next couple of days were horrendous in terms of disappointment and effectively mourning.'

Many of the 56 have been involved in local governance in some capacity. As a councillor, Alan was well prepared for generating a bit of clout in terms of his General Election 2015 profile: 'It also meant I had been involved in a number of campaigns previously. Additionally, I had the confidence [that] we had a good ambitious SNP administration that I was integral to. I used this as a demonstration of ambition for the area and Scotland generally.'

Alan's opposition in the General Election campaign was Labour's Cathy Jamieson who was a high profile former MSP and MP holding positions in the Scottish Parliament including Minister for Education and Young People in 2001 and then Minister for Justice in 2003. She also ran against Iain Gray in the Scottish Labour Leadership contest in 2008. Alan really enjoyed campaigning for the seat of Kilmarnock and Louden, especially with the additional help of new SNP members: 'As seemed to be the case across the country, we had so many more activists than in previous campaigns, especially the 2010 General Election, when it seemed difficult to motivate little more than the most hard-core of activists.'

'We undertook significantly more canvassing than before and had basically seven-day-a-week campaigning for a sustained period of time. There was some nervousness about going up against a senior Labour MP who was well known in the area and generally liked. However, we had won the 2007 and 2011 Kilmarnock and Irvine Valley Holyrood constituency, won the 2011 Cumnock constituency, as well as having SNP-led council administrations in 2007 and 2012. Therefore, it showed that the SNP could win, if voters were willing to change their Westminster voting patterns. The national swing that the opinion polls showed also provided further evidence of possible success that the local canvassing backed up.'

Alan explained why he thought these trends towards the SNP occurred: 'The seismic change in the number of SNP MPs at Westminster is, I believe, a culmination of events and attitudes. For a number of years it's been clear that people in Scotland have become disillusioned with the Labour Party. The SNP have also been able to demonstrate competence and ambition at Holyrood and local council level, so the constant 'SNP bad' message has no ring to it. I believe that the Labour Party in Scotland, as well as losing its way in general, have become too SNP-focused rather than ambitious for Scotland. People have also recognised that the Scottish Labour Party is subservient to the main Labour Party, so that has influenced voting patterns too. Clearly the catalyst for the dramatic change at Westminster has been the Referendum and the negative campaigning, whilst aligning with the Tories has changed the mindset of a number of people who previously would have voted Labour. The move to the right at a UK-level by Labour confirmed that if a party was going to be progressive and stand up for Scotland then the SNP was the logical choice. On top of this, many No voters, I believe, would have been disappointed by the negative campaigning of the Referendum and so were also willing to vote SNP.'

Now he is in Westminster, Alan is focussing his drive to help people while trying to make a difference in a number of ways. On the state of Westminster politics, he said: 'UK politics is about having an establishment, and what appears to be a past cover-up of scandals is indicative of this. The convergence of the three 'national' UK Parties in terms of policies takes away challenge and alternative thinking, which makes the SNP presence much more important.' He is also unimpressed with the archaic practices of the house: 'The out-dated practices are not something that I've got used to. Especially the braying noises and the no clapping rule that have been documented. There should be more respect [for] individual speakers. I also find the manual voting system of queuing up in lobbies immensely frustrating due to the time it takes, and the knowledge that electronic voting would be so much more efficient.'

Alan's ultimate goals include seeing an independent Scotland although he understands that 'the future direction would be up to the voting public'. He hopes that this Scotland would be one of 'progressive politics' with 'a welfare system that supports people, a fair tax system, higher employment, and a return of more skilled manufacturing and engineering jobs; a strong, free-at-point-of-use NHS, and free higher education'. Outside of politics, Alan enjoys camping, cooking and some walking with his family's black Labrador. Most prominent, however, is his dedication to his football team: 'My main hobby is watching Killie FC games. I have been a season ticket holder since I was eighteen, and started a supporters club back in 1990 that still limps along today.' Alan goes along to matches with his two sons, Kyle, eighteen, and Dylan, sixteen, and his parents, because 'football has always been about socialising with friends and family as much as the main event of watching the game'.

28. CORRIE WILSON
AYR, CARRICK, AND CUMNOCK

'For me it's not about politics, it's all about community representation,' is a statement that encapsulates Corrie Wilson's approach to her new role as the MP for Ayr, Carrick, and Cumnock. Corrie was born in Ayr and has lived there her whole life. After Corrie left school, she started working in the civil service, where she worked for twenty years. Corrie described her job: 'I addressed peoples' barriers to help them get back to work. That led me to my first point of understanding barriers and red tape, and understanding how people can't access things. At the same time, while working full-time, I used to do voluntary youth work. I worked with kids on the street [who] were totally disenfranchised. It's the same kind of red tape there that stopped people being able to move forward and find interests.'

She left the civil service to study Psychology at university before moving into the voluntary sector, where she was involved in everything from school boards to youth work: 'My job at this point was to work with families that were at risk of becoming homeless, and again, I saw more barriers. My outlook on life has always been to have a 'can do' attitude and when I'm working in these sorts of environments all I was hearing was 'you can't because'. I then went on to be involved on school boards while my kids were in school and I then became a police custody officer: the role of that job was to visit prisoners in police cells to check [that] they were okay and getting looked after properly. At that point I was involved in the community council. For my whole life it's been about community and what sort of part I can play in that community to make it better.'

'While I was in the civil service I wasn't part of any political organisation because, to be honest, that was just too much of a minefield. After getting out of the civil service I could start looking at being political again. That got to the point in 2012 where I was asked if I would consider standing for local election. I think my motivation was at that point, 'okay, I've worked with people and been frustrated – maybe I can go from the inside and change things'. For me it's all about being that community representative and getting the community's voice heard.'

Corrie ran South Ayrshire's Yes campaign for two years: 'The strange thing is, although everyone was extremely disappointed [after the Referendum], we had booked a party for the Friday night which we decided to hold anyway come hell or high water because we had worked extremely hard. I think that the party was the best thing we could have done because being with that group of like-minded people that night let us come out of the Referendum with a positive outlook about what was going to happen next. Little did we know that there would be this massive increase in membership towards the SNP, but we came out with the resolve to keep going forward. Not to mention the fact that we had become friends with people from all walks of life, who you might not have crossed paths with in normal day-to-day life.'

'I think that the Referendum showed that there was a bunch of people out there who cared about their community, country, and fellow citizens who wanted to make a better life. There were also people who did say 'well I'm alright, Jack, but there are people who are less fortunate and I would like to be part of making that change'. Also, in my adult life you only had the two main choices for Westminster: Tory or Labour. I think the mindset that created the Yes campaign was hope, and people latched onto that hope of finding a different way to do things. I think the politics that we have now is based on asking what we can do for each other and how we can make it a better place for living and working, not just about me, me, me. I certainly never had any interest whatsoever in becoming a Westminster politician. As the weeks progressed into months after the Referendum, you could see the change it had brought about. Being an MP for me is just the next thing that we have to do to work towards getting our voices heard.'

Corrie's years working for South Ayrshire council set her up for Westminster as she explained: 'For some bizarre reason South Ayrshire council's quarters is a very old building surrounded internally with wood panelling. In a way, I've just swapped one wood panelled workplace for another (obviously on a much grander scale). There is a bit of a culture shock though, going from a normal job to public service, which is done differently. [...] The whole [Westminster] thing is out of date and out of touch on a grand scale. It goes back to the question: why do we have to continue doing something just because it's been done that way for hundreds years? The processes are so lengthy as well and it takes twenty minutes to do a vote when you could be pressing a button or swiping a card. The processes are long and drawn out, and it's not fit for purpose.'

Since becoming an MP, Corrie has had to give up being director of the Ayrshire festivals Septembayr and Ayr Renaissance, but she still plans to be involved in the community. In any spare time she gets outside of her busy Westminster schedule she enjoys tracing her family tree and photography. On her inspiration, Corrie said: 'The one person that has inspired me though my life is a best friend of mine who passed away a couple of years ago. She fought with cancer five times and she never, ever, lost her spirit. I think from that point of view, to watch her battle time and time again and never lose that hope, coming back to hope, never losing that willingness to hope for something better is a huge inspiration to me. I had cancer myself in 2010 and she was an inspiration to me at that point as well.'

29. PATRICIA GIBSON
NORTH AYRSHIRE AND ARRAN

Patricia Gibson was born in and grew up in Govan, where she attended St Andrews Primary School, then St Gerard's secondary school. From there she went to study English at Glasgow University before becoming an English teacher, working in St Ninian's High School in Giffnock until the dramatic election this year which saw a swing of nearly thirty percent away from her Labour opponent.

Patricia became aware of political issues from an early age: 'I would say that I first became interested in politics during the miner strikes, the Thatcher era. When I was growing up, everybody voted Labour. Our job, the people in my community, was to turn up every five years, vote Labour, and then go home and forget all about it. When Thatcher was running the UK, having grown up in a very poor background, I looked around and I saw lots of people like me. Very few people manage to improve their circumstances and I realised that the only people who could stand up for Scotland were Scottish people – and Scottish people whose loyalty was to Scottish people – as opposed to the Labour party. We know from the Thatcher era that although Scotland overwhelmingly voted Labour, they were not able to protect Scotland. They weren't able to stop one factory from closing, they weren't able to save one job, and they weren't able to protect one family: only the Scottish people making their own decisions can do that.'

One of the most inspirational figures in Patricia's life is her mother: 'I think that I am emotionally quite strong in the face of adversity and I think that certainly a role model for how to keep on going when things get tough is my mother. My mother was widowed very young with eight children in what was, for her, effectively a foreign country, and that must have been a very isolating experience. She had [...] deep grinding poverty. I don't know how I would have coped with that but she just got on with it, and that is what I've learned from her: when things get hard, when things are tough, you just get on with it. You make the best of it that you can. But there have been so many positive influences in my life. My husband's an MSP, Kenneth Gibson, he's a great source of strength to me, a great support to me, the local SNP members in the constituency who have helped me through this campaign and who have worked very hard alongside me. In terms of this particular election and moving Scotland forward, Nicola Sturgeon, of course, is a huge asset to the party, a huge asset on the doorstep when you're out campaigning.'

Outside of politics Patricia enjoys reading, and is a big fan of Victorian literature, particularly Charles Dickens. On election night she reveals how reading was on her mind: I spared a wee thought [...] despite all the excitement and the sense of history unfolding before us [...] for Anthony Trollope, whose political novels I love, because although he had a prodigious talent and a prodigious output, [he] always felt very unfulfilled because, despite the fact that he was such a great writer, he felt that his destiny was to be in the House of Commons, and he never achieved that and never got over the disappointment of that.'

The 2015 General Election was not Patricia's first; she had stood in 2010 for the same seat, and prior to this she was a councillor in Glasgow, as well as the SNP spokesperson on education. She explained her experience of the 2010 election saying: 'In 2010 the SNP were squeezed out of the Westminster election narrative and our vote increased by 0.1%. In the seat where I stood it increased by 8% so we really bucked the trend so I knew then what we could do and I knew we were gaining ground and the whole narrative by 2015 had changed because of the Referendum. It was a seat for which I had been working the patch since 2010 and I knew there was more to be done. There was a big mountain to climb, obviously, and we chipped away at that in 2010 because we had a great team, and this time we managed to turn it right around.'

As with many of the 56 Patricia Gibson was heavily involved in the Scottish Referendum campaign. Following the No vote, Patricia said that she was 'Very very disappointed. I remember people were saying, pundits and people in the No campaign, what now for the SNP? Nobody could have predicted the huge surge in support for the SNP but the next morning I thought that our role had become a lot more important because promises were made and there is no doubt, [that] the people who were swithering were convinced by this rush of activity by the No campaign in the last ten days. So it was always going to be a case of trying to make sure that we extracted as much as possible for Scotland on the basis of these promises which were not worth the air that was taken to expel them into the ether. [...] I felt the way that so many people felt – that I wanted to use my disappointment and my frustration constructively. So what I did was, on the Sunday after the Thursday, I went out and put SNP leaflets in my community and I went out with the most garish, brightly coloured SNP bag you've ever seen in your life because I wanted people to know, even if I wasn't putting leaflets through their door, that I was from the SNP and I was out and I wasn't going away. Actually, the response from people that I met was really quite heartening, showing that defiance, the idea that we're not done, we're not finished, we're still fighting and we're not going away. I had people out walking their dogs, banging into lampposts, looking at me saying 'my God – SNP are out!' What does it take? And I think that's important because there are so many people who, for a variety of reasons, are not actively political, although they have strong views and strong opinions, and don't actively engage. They need those of us who are [political], to keep fighting for them as well, and they rely on us, the people who don't have a voice, people who don't feel confident or have the space in their lives or the resources or the means or have barriers to participation – they need to know that the fight goes on and that we continue to fight for the best deal for Scotland and the kind of society that so many people in Scotland aspire to.'

We then spoke about Patricia's focuses while at Westminster: 'I'm clearly interested in education, I've been an English teacher for over twenty years. I'm also interested in the constitution, I'm interested in bringing as many powers home to Scotland as possible. I believe that the only people who will make decisions in the best interest of Scotland are the Scottish people and they've mandated the SNP to do that, quite specifically in this election I think, and that's our job to make sure that we represent the values and interests and aspirations of the Scottish people, that's why we're here. I am also specifically against the welfare cuts: the twelve billion pounds of them. Also, any attempt to abolish the Human Rights Act must be resisted and I know that that's been kicked into the long grass for a while but I certainly wouldn't say it's gone away. Any attempt to drag Scotland against its will out of Europe would be strongly resisted. We have been told that we are an equal partner in a family of nations. Well, let's see how equal we are. There has to be a mandate from all parts of the UK for that to happen and Scots will take a very dim view if they vote to stay in but are taken out of Europe against their wishes.'

The ultimate goal for Scotland in Patricia's mind is independence: 'I don't know if that's going to be next year, [in] twenty years, forty years. [...] Obviously I would like Scotland to be independent as soon as possible, not for some abstract constitutional reason but because I honestly believe that the best way to improve people's lives is to create an equal, fair, and prosperous society [and] for Scotland to govern itself, just like a normal, ordinary country. There is no country that I know of who has won its independence and then thought 'we shouldn't have done that'. I just want Scotland to [...] take its place in a family of nations globally.'

30. PHILLIPPA WHITFORD
CENTRAL AYRSHIRE

Phillippa Whitford was born in 1959 in Belfast, where she lived until she was ten. Her early life was difficult for her mother because her father died a week before her third birthday, and despite not having 'a huge amount of anything', Phillippa remembers her childhood fondly because of the tight-knit community she lived in where 'everybody was always in everybody else's houses and there were lots of kids'. At the age of ten and around six months before the Troubles broke out, her family relocated to Dumfries.

Phillipa's stepfather's job meant that she lived in a number of places though her childhood: 'I had a few years in Dumfries, then we lived in Hartfordshire, and I went to school in North London. I used to commute into London every day which, as a twelve year old was pretty challenging, especially being right in the middle of the rail strikes in the 1970s.' Phillipa's family then moved to Glasgow where Phillipa finished school before enrolling at university in Glasgow. She later graduated with a degree in Medicine. Phillippa remembers being in medical school and speaking to the recently retired Medical Officer Harry Burns about wanting to specialise in surgery, to which he replied: 'Do you not realise that women can't do surgery?' 'It wasn't that he thought I couldn't do it, there were not senior women in surgery at this time at all,' she explained.

After Glasgow, Phillippa went to Belfast to complete her surgical training. She returned to Ireland because wanting to go home had always been at the back of her mind, and studying made this possible. She remembers writing a 'gee us a job letter', after which 'I think they interviewed me out of curiosity [...] I think they wanted to take a chance on me. When I started orthopaedics in Belfast I was the first woman they had ever had, and someone had obviously thought my name was a typo and changed it to Philip, so when it turned up I thought they might have a heart attack because they kept saying 'you can't be' and I kept saying 'of course I am'. It was obvious at the time that there were a few [women] at all trying to break through, and then there was a lot of talk over who might be the one to get into surgery. That was just an added pressure though, it wasn't why I was doing it.'

In 1991 Phillipa left Ireland to go to Gaza. She had always desired to do developmental work and she said that when she hit thirty she started to question if she was on the right path: 'I realised that if I was going to go overseas I needed to do it now.' Phillippa and her husband then spent a year and a half looking for an appropriate project while repeatedly ignoring an advert in the British Overseas Medical Service because, as Phillipa recalled, 'it just sounded too naff'. In the end she looked at the advert properly and saw it was advertising for a surgeon and an anaesthetist; the latter was an area in which her husband was training in at the time. She replied to the advert: 'When the letter came back describing the hospital in Gaza, I thought the job was bang on because I wanted to be able to teach and leave skills behind.' In 2010 Phillippa got the opportunity to go out to Jerusalem in the West Bank and spend time with one of the surgeons she had trained while in Gaza who was now consultant in Jerusalem: 'It was amazing to see the service he was providing.'

Phillippa has always been political, though stressed the fact that she had always been political with a small 'p'. 'The social justice agenda worldwide is really important to me and I'm the SCIAF (Scottish Catholic International Aid Fund) Ambassador for South West Scotland, so I had the chance to visit Kenya and Tanzania to visit

AIDS projects with them.' She joined the SNP in 2012, when it was clear that there was going to be a Referendum: 'I had always believed in Scottish independence, but I had never joined a political party because if you are a voter you should put the party through their paces every single time. They should not be allowed to assume they had your vote in your pocket. They should work for it. In the past, like everybody, I voted Labour for Westminster. I always voted SNP for Holyrood, but never voted for Labour after 2003 and the Iraq war. That was the end of them as far as I was concerned.'

Phillippa's next political move was during the Referendum. She explained that at the beginning of the campaign she 'had been doing what everyone else was doing'. When Yes Troon started in March 2013 Phillippa had spent her time standing at stalls and delivering newspapers. Then, at the beginning of 2014, she started holding public meetings to assist the formation of other groups in smaller villages. A critical moment for Phillippa was when Better Together published a leaflet in January 2014 stating that if Scotland became independent Scotland would leave the NHS: she realised that a lot of hospital staff might vote No because they believed this, without realising that the Scottish NHS has been separate since 1948 and the whole principle of the NHS was based on the Highlands and Islands medical service. This was when she started to talk about it.

She described the video that brought her in to the spotlight: 'It was on the 1st of May [and] I did a big Women for Independence cafe in Strathaven and some people asked if I minded them videoing the meeting, and I said it was fine. I thought that only six people would see it and I could show it to my mum, so thought nothing of it. I really didn't think of it having a huge effect, and then someone told me I had gone viral. So then just a couple of weeks later we kicked off NHS YES. After that I had so many requests from all over Scotland to speak, that together my husband and I travelled over 5,000 miles. This was all on top of my normal job and I didn't take any holidays.' Phillippa chose to work for independence alongside her necessary job because she 'thought it was just so crucial' and 'really really believed we should go for independence'.

After the Referendum it took two months to convince Phillippa to run as a candidate for Westminster. She was hesitant due to her job but as more and more people asked her it kept chipping away. Eventually Alex Salmond asked her to run at the autumn conference: 'I said the same to him – that I wasn't standing – and he said I needed to rethink that. I went home thinking, 'he was First Minister until yesterday, I will at least talk about it. But I am still not going to do it'. My husband had moved [his opinion] around 180 degrees and was now for me doing it.' About a week later Phillippa was running a rally for Women for Independence with Jean Freeman and there were well over one hundred women discussing how women must step forward and speak up in order to get involved in politics. The next morning Phillippa asked herself 'if not me who? [...] I can't say it was a decision taken rationally, but rather more emotionally motivated'.

Now down in Westminster, Phillippa has the very apt position of Health Spokesperson and she intends to constantly challenge the government while also standing up for ordinary people in England whose NHS is undermined. In her maiden speech she paid tribute to Scotland's health system saying, 'In Scotland after devolution we went back to our roots, got rid of trusts, and again became a single unified public NHS. That has allowed us to work right across our country in developing quality standards and improving safety. We have our challenges. The NHS in Scotland is not remotely perfect; we face the same challenges as the rest of the United Kingdom. But despite the quips that were made by the Secretary of State, it does come down to cooperation and not competition.'

31. STUART MCDONALD
CUMBERNAULD, KILSYTH, AND KIRKINTILLOCH EAST

At the age of thirty-six, Stuart McDonald is one of the younger members of the 56. Born in Glasgow, he grew up in Milton of Campsie where he lives now. He attended Kilsyth Academy, then studied at the University of Edinburgh, where he graduated, firstly, as a Bachelor of Law (hons), and secondly, with a Diploma in Legal Practice in 2001. While at the University of Edinburgh, Stuart studied European and Comparative Law on an ERASMUS year at the University of Leuven between 1997 and 1998.

Stuart then went on to work in law from 2001 to 2009. He secured several positions, including the role of Human Rights Solicitor. He then worked at the Scottish Parliament as a Senior Researcher in 2009 before leaving in February 2013 to become a Senior Researcher for the pro-independence Yes Scotland campaign, a position he held until the independence Referendum in 2014.

Stuart's engagement with politics started early, and he was particularly affected by the Thatcherite era: 'I remember when Mrs Thatcher was Prime Minister and you couldn't but be aware of the fact that she was so widely disliked in Scotland because she was imposing all sorts of fairly drastic policies. Even if you don't have a firm grasp of all the issues behind them – as you don't at that age – it's hard not to pick up on that basic almost injustice, that here we have a government doing all sorts of drastic things and that doesn't have a mandate in my country in Scotland.'

Stuart has been a member of the SNP for his whole life thanks to his parents: 'I've always been a supporter for the SNP for as long as I can remember. I never supported another political party. Both my mum and dad have always supported independence for Scotland. My mum has voted for different independence-supporting parties during a time, my dad's more of an SNP man. He never joined the party until I joined so I was following in their footsteps but was maybe motivated to go a bit further and be a bit more active than they'd ever been. But the starting point is definitely the political views of my parents.'

Stuart's passion for politics is matched by his passion for football: 'I love football, I've been a season ticket holder at Tannadice Park for many years. [...] I also play football and have played up until now for Scotland's first LGBT football club – 'Hot Scots Football Club' as they're known. That's been difficult as I hadn't missed a game for a couple of years, and I think I played sixty minutes last year altogether in a friendly. I'm getting a bit old for it now as my knees aren't that up to ninety minutes any more.'

After the Referendum Stuart was selected as the candidate for the Cumbernauld, Kilsyth, and Kirkintilloch East constituency and he then became the MP for the area. He attributes many reasons for his running as a parliamentary candidate to chance: 'I had been working full-time at Yes Scotland headquarters and I knew my contract was coming to an end on the 19th of September. I was living in Glasgow at the time. Because I didn't know what I was doing afterwards, regardless of the vote, I handed in my notice for my flat so I moved out and back in with my parents – where I still am, I'm afraid to say – so that was me back in my home constituency again. I was Julie Hepburn's Campaign Manager in 2010, they were first out the blocks to open up for nominations, so I think they were so fast that they got almost halfway through and nobody had put their name in. So one or two folk came to me and asked if I'd be interested and the more I thought about it the more I thought – why not? I've not got anything else to do just now and at that time I don't think anyone was predicting what would happen afterwards. There was still a possibility that this could be quite a difficult period for the SNP actually because we'd just lost the Referendum. If I'm brutally honest I thought it would take me up to May and life would turn back to some sort of normality, but it didn't really turn out like that!'

When asked why he thought the 56 were voted in with such a large majority, Stuart replied: 'There are probably all sorts of factors at play as to why the 56 were elected. The Referendum made a huge impact: the way that Labour acted throughout that. I'm sure they'll see now that it was a disaster to be walking so close to the Tories and pursuing a line which was largely so negative and appeared to be acting to protect vested interests without a positive vision. So much of it has to be the record of the SNP – people seem to like its approach to politics and the way it pursues its policies in government. Also, Scotland like a lot of the people that are involved in the SNP, and Nicola Sturgeon is clearly a very popular First Minister. There are all sorts of factors at play and it will take some time to work it all out.'

As an MP Stuart's focus will be on independence but also matters of social justice: 'If you listen to the maiden speeches [...] you'll see all sorts of common threads through them. Obviously we're all here because we believe in independence for Scotland and in maximising the powers that Scottish Parliament can have, but I don't think there's been a maiden speech so far that hasn't mentioned presence of foodbanks in the speaker's constituency [...] One of the first events I did after I became an MP was to go along to one of the local foodbanks. We did a collection – we did this twice during the campaign, we had Super Saturdays, as it became known – and members also had the opportunity to make donations to foodbanks and that got a fantastic response so I think, not just MPs but our activists generally are very motivated by issues of social justice and equalities and ensuring that work pays a fair wage. I'm also interested in issues of immigration and asylum, which is helpful given the spokesperson job. Having worked for three years as an immigration and asylum lawyer I'm quite motivated to combat some of the rhetoric and views that are held down in London.'

'I'm also really very passionately motivated to oppose the repeal of the Human Rights Act and all my colleagues in the justice policy team are really looking forward to that fight when it comes. Who knows, they [the Tories] might still chicken out, but I don't see how they could manage that, given their manifesto commitment. The ongoing cuts agenda – we'll have to look in detail at the immigration bill – but it looks like more tokenistic scapegoating nonsense in pursuit of an unachievable target.'

Many of the 56 believe in some fundamental differences between Scottish thinking and parts of the rest of the UK, but Stuart believes it's just a matter of perspective: 'Sometimes people point to these social attitude surveys but sometimes I think [that with] the questions [they ask], you could go right across Europe and you wouldn't see that much variation. 'Do you believe in a fairer society' – I mean, who on earth is going to say no? People in Scotland are a little bit different in the sense that they're interested in a different political party to achieve the goals. I'm sure people across the United Kingdom want to see a less unequal society, they want to see fairer wages, but people in other parts of the United Kingdom have repeatedly voted for centre right or right-wing parties to achieve these things, whereas people in Scotland are continuing to vote for centre parties or centre left parties, so that's where I think the difference comes in. It's just a different political outlook.'

In his maiden speech, Stuart referenced the humorous mishaps that have occurred due to his fellow SNP MP Stewart McDonald: 'The other major challenge that I have faced is the fact that there are two new SNP MPs called Stuart McDonald here in Westminster. Given that we spell our first names differently, I was expecting only the odd stray email or letter. In fact, in two short months, my honourable Friend the Member for Glasgow South (Stewart McDonald) has managed to steal my seat on one flight to Glasgow, leaving me stranded at Heathrow; cancel two other sets of return flights, hijack one of my constituents who had travelled 500 miles to lobby me; and steal credit in Hansard for my first ever intervention in this Chamber. At such times, many words spring to mind, but 'honourable' and 'Friend' are not among them.' Looking to the positive side, Stuart says 'it was however comforting to receive a note congratulating me on my maiden speech some four weeks before I rose to make it.'

32. MARION FELLOWS
MOTHERWELL AND WISHAW

Marion Fellows was born in Central Hospital, Irvine, in Ayrshire. She was brought up in Ayr where she attended Russell Street Primary School, Belmont High, and then Carrick Academy in Maybole. After school she went to Heriott Watt University where she studied Accountancy and Finance. Following her degree, she taught Business Studies at West Lothian College. Having lived with her family in Wishaw and Bellshill since the 1970s, she was elected in 2012 as a North Lanarkshire Councillor for Wishaw, and Marion was very active in in the Yes Motherwell and Wishaw campaign during the 2014 independence Referendum.

When Marion was young she was quite apolitical. Her father, however, was a cooperative milkman with strong political views: 'He started voting SNP in the sixties which is quite an unusual thing for a cooperator. One thing he was keen on was that people should think about what they're going to vote. Where he worked and where we lived, you voted Labour and that was it. My father taught me to think about what I was going to do, so after we came back from London [in the] mid seventies I started to really think about how I was going to vote and I voted SNP more or less always from then. But I wasn't an activist or even a party member, I just felt that way. I used to say I could never understand why the Maltese could vote for their own country and I couldn't – because people from Malta had independence and it was a tiny wee place – so I could never see the logic of why Scotland couldn't manage.'

Marion's journey into politics started later in life with her family helping to serve on a local scale: 'Although I had always been interested in politics, I first started really engaging with it when my eldest son did a Politics degree in Edinburgh and then went on to work for the SNP, and he came down to Westminster and worked with the MPs and became Chief of Staff, and then came back to Scotland in 2005 when Alex Salmond returned as leader. My son actually sent the local branch secretary round to sign me up because I [had] voted SNP for a long time.'

'I joined my local branch I think in 2003-4 and I'd never been able to join anything without getting involved, so became the branch Convener and I was branch Secretary. I stood against Jack McConnell in 2007 because in Motherwell and Wishaw it was a hopeless cause. Somebody had to do it, so I thought let's go for it. I increased our share of the vote and led the charge as I was the first vote to be announced.'

'Dame Shirley Williams was the first political person I ever heard speaking – about immigration to students – I think it must have been about 1970 at the University of Lancaster. My political inspirations are varied: folk like Winnie Ewing, Margo MacDonald, and our present First Minister. I think I have always been most impressed by people who were in politics and believed what they were trying to do – people like Tony Benn – sometimes I agreed with him, sometimes I didn't, but I admired his passion and [...] his commitment. Somebody like Tony Blair I felt was at the opposite end of the spectrum [who] would have changed his policies at the drop of a hat to get a few more votes.'

Marion's current political views are 'driven by a sense of fairness and justice. During the Yes campaign I realised how left of centre I am. I mean, I hadn't really thought about it. I was a committee trade unionist, I still am. EIS is sometimes not seen as a trade union per se, but I was in the College Lecturers Association and then the Further Education Lecturers Association and we had branch bargaining, so

I was heavily involved in negotiating, dealing with disputes, people being victimised, so equality is my watchword. [...] I don't think it's fair that the Tory party are imposing their will in Scotland when they only have one MP. That drives me forward.'

Marion was heavily involved in the Yes campaign for her area, and spoke about her feelings after the vote: 'I was gutted but actually it was easier for us in Motherwell and Wishaw than other places because we had voted Yes. If someone had told me six months out that they'd vote Yes in Motherwell and Wishaw and No in the rest of Scotland I'd have been amazed. The outcome overall was awful, not unexpected, but still a blow. In October and November when we started moving forward with the General Election campaign I met so many people who said 'I wish I had voted Yes'.'

Since Marion became an MP she has had to quickly learn the Westminster system because she is an SNP Whip: 'Westminster is a real old boys network and I think there are not very many ordinary working folk and you can say that I'm not an ordinary working person now but I came from a very staunch working-class background. My mother was a cleaner and my father was a milkman and for them education was the answer so my sister and I were educated out of where we were born because my parents saw that as the way forward. Even though we were two girls, I was the first member to go to university from my entire family in 1967. It was very unusual back then.'

'This isn't home, we're not here to settle down and that's the driving force. Parliament is a beautiful building, the staff are wonderful, a lot of very good work goes on here, but we're not here to make it last another thousand years, we're here so Scotland can break free and just be independent. It's not an anti-English thing at all, we just want what's best for us because a lot of the policies down here are focused on the majority and that's not Scotland.'

She comments further: 'I think we are much more egalitarian. We believe in the common weal and that it is your duty to help. Now, I'm not painting a rosy picture because not everybody feels exactly like this, but there is, all over Scotland, an idea that you help people rather than look down on them. When people are struggling you give them a helping hand. I think that ever since Maggie Thatcher did her Sermon on the Mound about there being no such thing as society – most people in Scotland would profoundly disagree with that.'

'My vision for Scotland is about my granddaughters and it's about the things we fought for during the Referendum campaign. It's about a fairer and more equal society, it's about looking after people, it's about having the powers to create jobs and to make life better for lots more people. I think that's really what I see happening. I think we would become a much more Scandinavian-type democracy.'

Outside of politics Marion has varied interests: 'I'm a passionate Scotland football supporter although my children won't go with me because I shout too much! I also really enjoy spending time with my granddaughters – I really miss them – and my husband and my cat. But actually I'm a demon knitter. [...] I think I've said jokingly that I'd like to start up an all-party parliamentary group on knitting. I do it to relax and when your hands are busy it frees up your brain. I also like to read and to travel.'

33. KIRSTEN OSWALD
EAST RENFREWSHIRE

Born in Dundee but raised in Carnoustie, Kirsten Oswald grew up by the seaside. Playing in the North Sea was a regular weekend activity for everybody, despite the cold: 'The cold isn't something that bothers you unduly, its character building,' she joked. 'If you waited until it was warm to go paddling you'd never go in, so you just did it.'

While Kirsten enjoyed the idyllic setting of the coast, her parents were not content with simply enjoying the scenery and having an easy life. Both strong believers in independence and the SNP, Kirsten's parents would often travel across the country campaigning for the party. When back at home they often engaged their daughters in political discussions but as Kirsten attests 'my parents made sure they never pushed their views on my sister and me'.

Politics was part of everyday life for Kirsten and when the opportunity arose to attend university she felt it was a natural choice to study Politics. She was, however, always keen to think ahead for the future, so she choose to study both History and Industrial Relations, believing that this combination would give her skills that would help her secure employment after university. The University of Glasgow accepted her to study a MA, but throughout her time at University she discovered that it was History rather than Politics that she found most enjoyable. As her honours years approached, she decided it was time to focus on one subject and she elected History for her single honours.

Kirstin found graduating from university a strange experience. Having always been busy – working paper rounds as a young girl in Carnoustie and in multiple student jobs while at university – after graduation she found that she now had to step into the real world of work and she wasn't sure how to do that: 'When I finished my final exams I didn't have a job yet [...] so I went to the job centre, as that's where I thought I'd get a job.' Her decision to speak with the job centre yielded a surprising result: the centre's manager offered her a job with the HR team on the spot. She jumped at the chance, hating the idea of being out of work with nothing to do after graduating, and the job centre seemed like the perfect opportunity to begin her working life.

After more work with the job centre, her university background in Industrial Relations started to become much more helpful than anything she had learnt in Politics or History: '[The job] really got me interested in the employment side of business,' she recalled. The position in the job centre gave Kirsten the opportunity to find her feet in the HR world, which convinced her that this was the area in which she wanted to foster her career. She left the job centre after only six months, because she had secured a job with a bigger firm's HR department.

Kirsten and her family then moved to Clarkston, where life centered upon her family and her career and politics seemed like a distant memory. Even when her mother became the Provost of Angus Council Kirsten could not be convinced to join the SNP. It all changed, however, when the Referendum became a reality after the 2011 Scottish elections, as Kirsten explains: 'I remember thinking, why am I not a member [...] when [the Referendum] is going on? I can't sit back, I absolutely need to be a part of this.'

Believing that a Yes vote in the Referendum was about to happen, Kirsten joined her local Women for Independence group in Clarkston and finally joined the party in 2014, much to her parents' surprise. September however dealt a devastating blow to Kirsten in her first political campaign, unlike her parents who had been used to witnessing defeat over the years. As the party in East Renfrewshire started to become flooded with new members, Kirsten had renewed hope: that while the campaign was over, the debate was not.

When nominations opened for candidates to stand in the election Kirstin did not initially go forward: 'I am not really a risk taker,' she said. Yet her fear of risk could not stop the overwhelming excitement that the possibilities of standing for election offered: 'It seemed to me if I didn't do this now I would regret it. I was on a forward trajectory in my own head, and so politically engaged. I didn't want the momentum to stop.' Despite only being a party member for less than a year, she won the selection contest to go up against the Scottish Labour Party's leader Jim Murphy in the General Election.

The campaign was exhausting and it was often under the national media spotlight due to the SNP's potential to deal a massive blow to the Labour Party. For Kirsten, however, it wasn't about anyone else but herself and her campaign: 'I didn't see myself as looking to take a scalp, it couldn't be about [Jim Murphy]. [...] I really thought I could do a good job for East Renfrewshire. I could only concentrate on me and my campaign.'

When election night arrived it was a tense affair for Kirsten: national polling had shown the seat to be an extremely close race, and throughout the campaign the canvassing had revealed the same. When the ballot boxes started to be counted and as the night progressed, it began to appear more and more likely that it would be an SNP win: 'The closer we got to the day I didn't think it was going to happen,' she later admitted. 'But on the night, I had a strong indication from within the room quite early in the evening [about] which speech I would be using.' It was the victory speech and results showed a massive 24.3% swing towards the SNP which saw Kirsten unseat the Leader of the Scottish Labour Party.

Kirsten's rise to political prominence has been meteoric, much like the rise in support for the SNP in her own constituency. Now a member of the SNP's Westminster Executive as well as a spokesperson on the Armed Forces and Veterans, Kirsten has become a senior figure in the party. Her roots still remain as that young girl growing up on the coast of the North Sea and the ideals her parents taught her of fairness and equality still ring true: 'People need to get a fair crack at the whip. It can't be all about the 1%, we need to think about the other 99%. Things are so diverse between the top and the bottom of society, and we need to normalise that.'

34. ANGELA CRAWLEY
LANARK AND HAMILTON EAST

Born in Bellshill in 1987, Angela grew up in Hillhouse, where poverty and deprivation surrounded her childhood: 'I don't remember my childhood being totally defined [by poverty],' she remarked, 'although I do remember that my family would sometimes struggle to put food on the table.' At school, by the end of fourth year, most of her fellow classmates did not stay on to study their Highers and going to university was not a common plan. Yet Angela was convinced that education would enable her to succeed in life, and she became set on going to university. Angela was eventually accepted to study Politics at the University of Stirling. Despite not feeling like a very political person, Politics was the first choice for Angela because the prevailing memory of inequality from her childhood had left her with deep questions about the society around her; by understanding the system, she might have answers to those questions.

During her first year at Stirling Angela became immersed in political campaigns. Her university bedroom was plastered with posters of campaigns against the student endowment fee put in place by the Lib-Lab Scottish Executive at the time. This period also provided a political awaking for Angela and she started to shift her allegiance towards the SNP before finally joining the party at the end of her first year: 'I did study Politics but I didn't want to necessarily go into politics once I graduated,' she said.

After finishing university Angela wanted to travel and she secured employment with an educational travel company. She spent time in both mainland Europe and the United States 'expanding her horizons' while trying to find out exactly what she wanted to do in the future. On returning to Scotland, the opportunity to work in the Scottish Parliament was too much to turn down for a Politics graduate: she worked for Bruce Crawford then Clare Adamson, and following the 2011 Scottish Elections, Angela became more and more involved with the SNP and politics throughout Scotland. Through being so heavily involved in the 2011 elections campaigning around Lanarkshire, Angela became a natural candidate for council elections in Hamilton, but this was never the plan: 'I didn't ever see myself becoming a politician [...] but it was people like Clare Adamson and Bruce Crawford encouraging me to stand for councillor that convinced me to do it.'

Standing for the council election and fighting against three incumbent councillors was a daunting task for Angela. However she was elected on the first ballot with over 20% of the vote, beating both the Labour and Conservative parties: 'Being elected to council was probably one of the best experiences of my life,' she later said on being elected. The SNP failed to make enough gains on the council and instead they remained in opposition to a Labour minority administration in South Lanarkshire.

Failure to capture the council did not stop Angela's – or the SNP's – belief that as the Referendum approached there was a real chance that the area could vote Yes. Instead, South Lanarkshire delivered a resounding No vote, motivating Angela to stand for Westminster: 'I have campaigned most of my life against things that Westminster represents. But when we lost the Referendum I thought, if we've got to be part of Westminster then I want to work actively to get the best deal for Scotland.'

The next move was simple as Angela decided to seek election for the seat of Lanark and Hamilton East for the SNP. The election ahead turned out to be gruelling, but it was the story of Winnie Ewing, who had captured part of her constituency in the famous Hamilton by-election long before, that kept pushing her forward: 'When I was on the doorsteps it was amazing how many people still remember that election. Winnie Ewing really was a trail blazer for so many women in the SNP and I was definitely inspired by that and even today people in the constituency still remember her.' Much like Ewing, her task in the election would seem insurmountable: Angela was up against Jimmy Hood who, with a majority of over 13,000, had been elected as an MP in 1987, only eight days after she was born. Yet on election night, Crawley would achieve the seemingly unthinkable and take the seat with a majority of 10,100 votes. Her younger brother, who on the night had been sampling ballot boxes and knew the likelihood of the result, leapt in the air to celebrate when the election was announced. 'We took our message beyond our sphere,' she said of the campaign. 'We weren't just talking to ourselves and we offered a positive message of hope to the people of Scotland.'

Following in the footsteps of her political hero, Angela caused an early storm at Westminster speaking more times in the House of Commons in ten weeks than her predecessor had done in his past five years in Parliament. Her maiden speech, echoing the achievements of now former Scottish political champions Charles Kennedy and Margo MacDonald alongside promising to stand up for her constituents, was widely praised. It was her final words that left her mark on the chamber, much like Winnie Ewing had done many years ago: 'Let us, this term, make history. Let us collaborate and work together to represent with compassion, aspirational ideals and progressive politics. The people of Scotland voted loudly and clearly for an alternative to austerity. My team of fifty-five colleagues and I will work tirelessly with those on the opposition benches to ensure that we see an alternative to the damaging cuts to our public services.'

35. PHILLIP BOSWELL
COATBRIDGE, CHRYSTON, AND BELLSHILL

Phil Boswell was born and raised in Coatbridge, the area he now represents in the Houses of Parliament: 'When I came into the world the area was in decline already. Growing up in the area you could see the impact of poverty, you could see factories going quieter, and I had a friend called Hugh who used to walk from Sikeside to the SSE, Scottish Power, round about where St Augustine's Primary is. He used to walk past wire works and factories and engineering shops, all places you could get an apprenticeship in – you do that [walk] now and there's absolutely nothing.'

Phil, one of six siblings, was born in Bellshill Maternity in 1963 and went to school in the Coatbridge area. After school he started studying mechanical production engineering in Hamilton with the intention of getting a good job locally, but due to the decline of industry in the area over half of his fellow students left. Phil remembers at the time 'Lamburton were downsizing and Ravenscraig was closing, there was a big move away from heavy industry. Industry is what we were brought up on and it was all starting to disappear.' After Hamilton, Phil went on to undertake a degree in Quantity Surveying in what is now Glasgow Caledonian University. He chose this subject because his family owned a construction firm in Coatbridge that his brother, Jamie, now runs. However, the family business was hit by economic downturn, and Phil left because he had qualifications and was therefore the most likely of the brothers to find employment elsewhere. In fact, 'of the six siblings, five of us had to leave for work because of the lack of opportunity. You would work and your job would finish and you would get paid off and just to get a better chance we left. Some of us travelled around the world, most of us came to London and other parts of the UK. Jamie was the only one who didn't leave.'

After leaving the family business, Phil went into construction. From there he was at the Rosyth Royal Dockyard and worked for some quantity surveying firms in Glasgow. Yet the market for tenement refurbishments started to decline in Glasgow and the work began to dry up, so Phil decided to travel around the world in pursuit of work.

Phil worked in construction around the world and eventually started working for the oil and gas industry. He explained, however, that his family accompanied him for each move to a different country: 'When I've travelled I've always taken my family with me, originally with construction to Kuala Lumpar and Hong Kong. There's a culture in the oil industry of the guy going away to work and the wife staying at home with the kids, but I think that makes you grow apart and it didn't suit me, so Anne has come with us and the kids have come with us. I was in America as well.'

Phil went on to talk about the importance of his family now he works as an MP: 'Being an MP is a job and that's what people forget. With the amount of time I've spent in the oil and gas sector, this is a job where I'll be spending more time with my kids. Kyle's nineteen, Molly's fifteen, and Daisy is nine, and I haven't been around as much I would like to have been and I don't want to make that mistake again. I've got to be truthful, I know you can have that grandiose self-sacrifice thing with this job and I have sacrificed a lot, but I'm not sacrificing my family.'

Phil switched from the lucrative oil and gas sector to politics due to the problems he could see in Scotland: 'I left mechanical engineering as there seemed to be no future in it and they didn't tell me about oil and gas in Aberdeenshire over at Hamilton College but when I look back at it I think that we could have made a much better deal of things if people were told about what Scotland has to offer.'

One of Phil's motivations is to fix the inequality in Scotland while maintaining a strong economy: 'We are pragmatic in Scotland: while we're left and I've always been left, I'm not a communist. I believe that people should be rewarded and there's nothing wrong with paying someone more than someone else if you've earned it. The world we live in is very materialistic, but we shouldn't be frightened to reward hard work. I'm under no illusions: I'm part of a group of people who are doing politics for the right reasons. I don't know anybody yet who is in the mainframe style of politics and doing it for themselves. This is where my old party – the Labour party – fall down badly and have done for quite some time.'

When asked about the impact of the Referendum on Phil he replied: 'Well, there was a healing process as some of my family voted No, and I was – shall we say – not very nice about it. It was difficult. There was hollowness and frustration that we felt as we had done our politics. People who did their homework invariably voted Yes. It's obvious when you scratch the surface. We happen to be one of the wealthiest nations on earth so the economic argument was never really an issue for me. It fundamentally came down to the fact that people who don't share the same values are ruling us. I see England moving to the right, which saddens me. I have lots of relations down here [in England] who were disappointed that we didn't make the change that Britain needs.'

Phil switched from Labour to the SNP because of two main reasons. The first was a speech by Jimmy Reid in 2006 in which he said: 'Labour no longer represent the values I hold dear and was brought up in.' This 'made a big impact' on Phil and made him 'think about things'. Secondly, what solidified Phil's political change were some of his experiences working for the oil and gas industry: 'I'm still in confidentiality agreements with this, but I can speak generally. The numbers that are generated within the industry are not the numbers released through Westminster. What you get is projects, say, in the North Sea, operating from Aberdeen, passing information to London and this goes to the department of Energy and Climate Change then further on to Westminster. What I've seen in projects, and in projects in the public domain, do not add up to the figures that have been released – I can't say any more than that, but that made me angry and I know from the McCrone report that this has been going on for some time and I am witness [to] and part of the continuation of that, and that angered me. I wanted to do something about that and got involved in the SNP and the Referendum campaign.'

'I woke up to the Labour party moving to the right before most of Scotland and [I] wanted to see what was beyond the shallow meaningless platitudes designed to make you think that Labour are of the left. You wave a red flag and sing a song and talk of being the 'people's party' – that's not what matters to me and I'm not a fan of X-Factor politics. The people behind the policies and the people that make it work are what really interest me.'

I asked Phil what he is like as a person and what interests him outside of politics: 'Well, [...] I am a traditional Scottish and Irish folk singer. I suppose I'm a bit frivolous, irreverent, and downright rude, sometimes but fun – I take the piss basically. I push it too far sometimes, but I'm generally quite self-effacing. I can be pig-headed sometimes wrapped up in things – human! Normal! Like normal people are. There is a happiness in being true to yourself.'

36. NEIL GRAY
AIRDRIE AND SHOTTS

Born in 1986, Neil Gray is another younger member of the 56. Gray was born and brought up in Orkney where he attended a small primary school: his P7 class had just three other pupils. Neil is proud to be Orcadian and speaks positively of his upbringing on the islands: 'While Orkney is remote and has its challenges it is a great place to grow up because there is very little crime, good schools, and plenty of safe open spaces. Some of my family still live there and I visit when I can.'

Neil's engagement with politics started on Orkney: 'I've always been interested in politics and current affairs. We used to watch the news as a family and I was encouraged to have my own views on things. My dad was a member of the local school board and fought a successful campaign with other parents to keep our wee school open and eventually get a new one built. That type of local community activism has stayed with me.'

Politically engaged in his youth, Neil also advocated independence while at school: 'I remember being the only advocate for Scottish independence in my history class when I was fifteen or sixteen. I just saw it as being natural for a nation to govern itself. When I was thirteen I was chosen to carry the Orkney banner at the school parade for the re-opening of the Scottish Parliament in 1999. I felt so proud to be there and to be part of the day, but also wondered why we didn't have a Parliament before then, so I have supported what the SNP stands for from a young age.'

Neil left Orkney to attend the University of Stirling, where he graduated in 2008 with a Bachelor of Arts honours degree in Politics and Journalism. When asked if he had intended to go into a career in politics before university, Neil replied: 'No, I don't think you can plan a career in politics. At various stages I wanted to be a lawyer, a vet, a police officer, and a professional athlete. My first employment was in journalism and I was very close to pursuing that as a career as well. My degree actually started with studying Psychology and Sport Studies, but I changed modules to Psychology, Journalism, and Politics after the first semester before focusing on Politics and Journalism for the Honours year. I have always been interested in politics and at that time saw journalism as being the profession I would make a career from.'

After university Neil worked as journalist for the BBC and local newspaper titles before eventually moving to the SNP's press and research office in Holyrood. Following his time in Holyrood Neil was employed by Alex Neil MSP in his constituency office in August 2008 and became his office manager in 2011. Neil stated that leaving university 'at the right time' really helped his journey into the world of work: 'I was very fortunate that I found work quite quickly [...] A lot of my friends who graduated the following year, in the recession, found it far more difficult even though they were just as qualified as I was.'

Neil's experience of the independence Referendum campaign was 'energising'. He worked in varying degrees in the local campaigns in North Lanarkshire, West Lothian, and in Orkney. Neil shared some of his enthusiasm for the campaign: 'The Yes campaign was hugely uplifting to be part of and the street events, public meetings, and online activity that I helped to organise felt like we were part of a real political movement. I think the Referendum politically energised Scotland. The rise of social media has also helped voters access their politicians easier, and also access information, which allows them to cut through the spin. I don't believe there is a more politically aware electorate anywhere in these isles than in Scotland.'

When the results of the Referendum campaign came in, however, Neil was totally 'devastated' and he 'didn't move much from the sofa on the 19th through physical and emotional exhaustion. I really thought we could do it on polling day, right up until the first boxes opened so the result was even harder to take. But then I resolved in my mind that we were going to get our chance again and we would have a far smaller gap to narrow so we had to just keep going. Scotland will be an independent country, but we still have hard work to do to get there.'

Having worked for Alex Neil MSP for a number of years in his Airdrie and Shotts constituency, Neil knew the community well. He also saw Neil as an inspiration in his campaign, stating in a recent interview; 'If I can be half the man that Alex is then I'll be doing well in life. If I can be half the politician that he is then I will be representing the community well.' After being selected as a candidate Neil ran a campaign which he described as 'very positive'. He said: 'My fellow candidates in Airdrie and Shotts ran a positive campaign too and it was a pleasure to be part of [the process]. Our canvassing was showing us ahead from early on, but I always thought things would narrow as polling day approached. That meant we worked hard right up until the last voter cast their ballot and that work ethic paid off. I am incredibly proud to represent the good people of Airdrie and Shotts.'

When asked why he thought that the Scottish people elected the 56 to represent Scotland for this parliament, Neil outlined two reasons: 'One: the SNP gave the most inspiring pitch to the electorate about a different politics being possible and alternative to the cuts. Two: there was a general distrust in the establishment after the Referendum campaign. The SNP was seen as the most competent and best vehicle to stand up for Scotland.' Since going to Westminster, Neil has been placed on the Finance Committee and the Joint Committee for the Restoration and Renewal of the Palace of Westminster. Neil's main focus as an MP in the House of Commons is to achieve fairness, which he will push in committees as well as being part of the Social Justice team for the SNP Westminster group. He said: 'We don't live in a fair society in the UK. The rich are getting richer while the standard of living for those more disadvantaged is not improving. There is little fairness in the way we support people with disabilities and I don't believe the current political situation is fair. Scotland did not vote for a Tory government and yet we have them imposing deep cuts to our public services and denying us the powers promised to us and supported by 95% of Scottish MPs. Aside from being part of the Social Justice team for the SNP Westminster Group I will also be working on the ridiculous Palace of Westminster restoration proposals. I don't think we should be writing a blank cheque rising to billions of pounds for Westminster, while billions gets cut from disability welfare support.'

'The institution [of Westminster] is archaic, out of touch, and doesn't represent the people. There are some very good people working there – both MPs and the staff who serve the House of Commons – but the establishment is quite happy keeping things the way they have always been, which is great for tourists, but not so good for the public or for efficient and effective democracy.'

In his maiden speech in the Commons, Neil paid tribute to the constituency: '[Airdrie and Shotts] is a constituency dominated by heavy industry. Communities have literally been forged by mining, steel, and iron. The grit, determination, and common weal needed for workers, their families, and communities to make ends meet has lived on from those days and I am proud to represent people who are warm, generous, and welcoming.'

37. JOHN NICOLSON
EAST DUNBARTONSHIRE

Born in Glasgow in 1961, John Nicolson's family story is fascinating. On his father's side he descends from islanders: his father's family is from the Isle of Harris on one side and the Island of Orkney on the other. On his mother's side, he descends from shipyard workers and domestic servants in Govan. John, from a young age, was proud to learn about his family history through stories: he heard how his great, great grandfather had served as a church minister on the Isle of Harris and about his mother's father who died in the Clydeside Blitz when she was just twelve. All these tales were important to John because they gave him a sense of who he was and where he had come from.

Both his parents dreamt of attending university but they were forced to leave school at a very young age because they needed to work: their families lived in poverty and every wage counted. John remembered the importance that his parents placed on academic learning: 'My mum and dad used to say to me growing up that they didn't care what I did, so long as I went to university. They didn't care if I became a doctor, a lawyer or a musician, they didn't mind – they just wanted me to go to university.'

His father unfortunately did not live to see his son attend university, passing away just before John sat his Higher exams. Despite these adverse circumstances, John achieved top marks and went on to be accepted to study at multiple institutions: 'I wanted to get away from home and study Law [at the University of Edinburgh], because you're never really independent if you're living at home with your parents. When my dad died, I didn't feel I could leave my wee brother on his own with my mum, so I decided to go to Glasgow instead.'

Although he was accepted to study Law at the University of Glasgow, he decided to study English Literature and Politics instead, feeling that it would suit him better. His decision to study Politics led him into the bear pit of Glasgow University's student debating, where he excelled: John went on to become the Scottish Debating Champion and win the Observer Mace, before going to Princeton in the United States to win the World Student Debating Championships with his debating partner Frank McKirgan. At the World Championships, John and his partner had to convince an American audience that America should apologise for the American Revolution. Recalling the final debate John said: 'I argued that the American Revolution was the fault of Westminster and the Establishment, and that, had they handled the American's legitimate grievances better, it would have been unnecessary to take up arms. I argued that the armed insurrection was a tragedy that caused a lot of loss of live, and that voting with me meant they were actually voting to condemn the British Government.'

John's success at debating led him on to chair the BBC series *Mr Speaker Sir*, a show that paired famous personalities with student debaters and then pitted themselves against each other in a debate broadcasted from Glasgow University Student's Union. 'It was a bit of a hit,' recalled John. 'I used to go to the supermarket, and people would shout at me, 'Mr Speaker Sir!'.' John stopped taking part in the series when he graduated from university in 1984, and was awarded both the Kennedy Scholarship and Harkness Fellowship to study at Harvard the following year. John was accepted to study either at Harvard Law or with the Kennedy School of Government. Fascinated by the opportunity, he chose to study at the Kennedy School. Alongside the academic opportunities, the scholarship funded travel during the summer between the two years of study, and he chose to repeat the route of his fellow Harkness scholar Alistair Cooke. This route took him all the way through the Deep South of America, which he describes as 'the most amazing trip. I saw areas that had seen little change since slavery.'

When his time at Harvard was coming to a close, John considered trying to stay on and study the ever-elusive Law degree. Around that time he was taken to dinner by one of the trustees of the Harkness Fellowship Howard Simons, the editor of the *Washington Post* during the Watergate scandal who 'took a shine' to John and had 'acted as a mentor' to him. Simons informed John that a Senator was about to advertise for a young staffer in his office in Washington DC, and that he was willing to be John's reference for the job. The Senator in question was Daniel Patrick Moynihan of New York, and without hesitation John discarded the idea of Law and applied for the job: 'I flew down to Washington and went from one room to the next room until I got to the Senator's office and he sat down and interviewed me about my views on American Politics and knowledge of American Politics. Then at one point he started talking to me about Scotland and he had a detailed knowledge of Scottish Nationalism – he was an eclectic intellectual figure.'

John got the job and worked as a speechwriter for the Senator until 1988 when he was lured back to Scotland with the offer of presenting a new show called *Open to Question* on the BBC: 'I got a call out of the blue from this guy, David Martin, who said he'd like to buy me a ticket to fly back to Glasgow because he had a proposition [...] I found myself maybe a fortnight later in a studio with Archbishop Tutu live by satellite from Johannesburg, Donald Woods, who wrote *Cry Freedom* in the studio, and an audience of about fifty people. I had an earpiece in my ear and David Martin saying to me, "Now we are going to go out live. I want you to read the autocue, listen to my countdowns, speak when I say 'live', steer the discussion, and don't make any mistakes because the satellite is only up for thirty minutes".' John would later say that had he been more experienced in TV then he would have been 'petrified', but at the time for a young man it seemed like a huge amount of fun.

This programme was the start of John's career in both television and with the BBC. After *Open to Question*, John was recruited to become a political reporter for *On the Record* in London, before going on to report for *Panorama, Public Eye, Newsnight* and then host the BBC's *Watchdog* spin off *Health Check*. John then went on to become a presenter for *BBC News 24*, and was the news anchor on air when the Twin Towers were hit in 2001. Recalling the events he said: 'When I finally went off air and went home, I remember sitting at the kitchen table and just looking at the on-going news coverage and crying. The sheer sadness of it, and in particular the people jumping and the sheer desperation they must have felt in doing that.'

When John left the BBC he was given his own weekend breakfast show on ITV. He also hosted his own show on LBC Radio and became more involved in print journalism. Leaving the BBC had also enabled him to become more involved in the SNP, a party he had joined when he was only sixteen years old. When the Referendum came around, John, like so many others, gave up the time to canvass and deliver leaflets. His previous experience in journalism and speech writing led him into being brought onto Alex Salmond's debating team following the perceived victory of Alistair Darling in the first debate. It was on John's advice that Alex Salmond would, in the second debate, come out from behind his podium and speak to the crowd: 'It is an old trick from American politics, that you come out from behind the lectern and address the audience. I reckoned that Alistair Darling would not be comfortable enough to copy Alex Salmond when he realised it, and he wasn't. He just stood rigidly behind the lectern.'

Following the Referendum, John was asked to chair Nicola Sturgeon's tour of Scotland, including the incredible sell-out event at the Hydro arena. At this point the idea of entering electoral politics wasn't in his mind: like many others he still felt bereaved after the Referendum, and the idea of running headfirst into another election wasn't appealing. It was a meeting in his garden with the former MSP Andrew Wilson and Duncan Hamilton that eventually convinced John to stand for election, and he was selected to fight his home seat of East Dunbartonshire.

The campaign received a massive amount of attention from the Liberal Democrats, hoping to keep the seat with Jo Swinson having become a major player in the party over the course of the coalition.

'I wanted to fight a positive [campaign] that made people realise the benefit of voting SNP,' John later said. 'What you want to do is inspire people with what politics can achieve.' On election night the SNP would come from fourth in the previous election to win the seat.

Now in Westminster, John will likely look to his many heroes for inspiration on how to perform his duties as an MP. The one person that had the most profound effect on him and who was the reason that he joined the SNP was Margo MacDonald. John recounted the story that Margo told him before she died: 'when she was a young schoolgirl, she had dyed her new pair of white patent shoes black in order to meet Princess Margaret who was attending her school. She hadn't wanted to dye her shoes, but did so at the instance of her teachers. Princess Margaret both ignored her and her shoes.' Margo told John that it was at that point she knew to 'never again compromise with the establishment'. More than anything else, John will likely hold that principle dear.

38. JOHN MCNALLY
FALKIRK

Before the 2015 election, John McNally was a well-liked local councillor. He is now an MP in the former Labour stronghold of Falkirk. Born in 1951, John grew up locally in Denny, where he attended primary school. Later he went on to St Modan's Catholic High School in Stirling. John has lived in the area his whole life, and became the local councillor in the 2005 Herbertshire by-election after taking a safe seat from Labour with a 24% swing to the SNP, becoming the region's first SNP councillor. Since then, the SNP has topped the poll in Denny and Banknock in the 2007 and 2011 Scottish Parliamentary Elections, and again in the 2007 and 2012 local elections.

John's interest in politics began around twenty years ago: 'I was probably originally a natural Labour supporter but they deserted us, we didn't desert them. The reason I became a councillor was because I wanted to change my local area. I've run my own hairdressing business for around forty years and I've had three salons, I'm now just quite happy with a barber shop that I work in, which is the greatest way in the world to keep in communication with your local people.' John's political views were also influenced in a very local way: 'I would say probably my own family were of immediate influence on me, especially my dad. Up to the modern day I would say my own local councillors here have been most influential in everything that I've managed to achieve. They've been the guiding light, particularly David Alexander.'

The 2015 General Election was the second parliamentary election that John McNally has stood in: the first was in 2010 when he went up against Eric Joyce, who was the MP in Falkirk from the 2000 by-election until 2015. Joyce had been a Labour MP until he left the party in 2012, after pleading guilty on charges of assault as well as a number of other incidents; he then continued to serve in Falkirk as an independent MP. The 2015 General Election saw a 24.1% swing from Labour to the SNP. John states that his main aim while serving as an MP currently is 'to return Falkirk to a decent, distinguished name that's well represented and that people associate with their politicians. I'll do that by working for my community as best as I can and let people have a belief again that we are here to serve and work for people.' John states that his father has been the most influential figure in his life as he 'was a decent, straightforward, honest man'.

John also wants to fight against Tory policies: 'I believe in the convention of human rights and also oppose the austerity cuts, as they're a major thing that will impact on everyone and everybody. As a councillor, up until a few weeks ago, we're continually fighting cutbacks that are impacting local people. I know that I've been involved in foodbanks and if you want to see what's happening, just go to your local foodbank and you'll see decent people coming along with their families – it's almost humbling to watch these people. It can't be just food though, I've worked with some charities, I guide people along to them so it's things like a bed, a heater, blankets: day-to-day things that most people don't really think about.'

Like many of the 56, John was involved in the Referendum campaign though after the No result he wasn't as heavily impacted as many of the other MPs: 'Three weeks before it, you could see that the writing was on the wall when they were coming out with so many promises. When the bid came out I thought, 'well, they're going to have to live up to this, one way or another'. I wasn't as disappointed because I knew that, somewhere along the line, things were going to have to change, because they will be brought to account – and they were backsliding immediately. When Mr Cameron stood on the doorstep it was almost a JFK moment, as we hadn't stopped counting the votes. The votes were still being counted in the Referendum and he stood on the doorstep of Number 10 and mentioned English Votes for English Law. I can honestly tell you this, without a word of a lie, I thought – we've just recruited some new members – but I had no idea that it was going to be like this. The lazy thinking days of just putting your X beside Labour have gone. People are more educated – they're brighter and they've got a good nose.'

'As well as this, I think that people associated with us, the SNP. And of course, the Labour Party have deserted people. They haven't worked for their local community. I think people have seen that Alex Salmond brought us to there and Nicola Sturgeon has taken it a step further. She talks in plain, simple language that people understand.'

He further stated: 'I think independence is far more likely to happen now. It's almost like it's taken the party eighty years since it formed to become an overnight success. We're definitely going into a period of change; whether we end up with an independent Scotland or an independent British Isles parliament, or a federal state, or whatever [...] things have changed and will keep changing – and of that I have no doubt. I want to see Scotland happier and healthier. I want to see youngsters coming up and being educated. I want to see decent entrepreneurs coming through, running their own businesses. I want to see us looking after people that can't look after themselves, and that is the mark of civilisation. I think this is an exciting time in political history. We don't really know where it's going yet but I don't see us moving back the way, and I think that you'll see – in two or three years' time – other political parties forming around the British Isles, joining together to cut out this metronome of Tory, Labour, Tory in Westminster completely.'

39. MARTYN DAY
LINLITHGOW AND EAST FALKIRK

Linlithgow and East Falkirk was a key seat for the SNP, and Martyn Day was selected with the tough job of beating Labour's Michael Connarty, who held a seat in the area since 1992. Yet Martyn won the seat in the General Election with an impressive majority of nearly 13,000 votes. Martyn is a well-known local councillor and campaigner and has lived in the area for most of his life: born in Falkirk in 1971 then moving to Linlithgow for school, he lived there until his election this year. At school Martyn was very interested in history and he found Thomas Paine an influential figure. Despite enjoying school, particularly history, Martyn did not go on to higher education: 'I left the school on the Friday and started work at the Bank of Scotland on the Monday, so I went straight from school into a career.'

Although Martyn has 'always been a believer in independence' he was not always actively involved. Martyn stated he 'was a cultural nationalist long before I became a political one' and it was this cultural nationalism that led Martyn into politics. While attending various heritage groups Martyn met Billy Wolfe who had formerly been the parliamentary candidate for West Lothian (the seat that became Linlithgow and East Falkirk) at the 1964, 1966, and 1970 General

Elections. Meeting Billy 'prompted me to become more of a political nationalist and I joined the party when I was eighteen, but it was a couple of years before I actually did anything!' In his speech following his election to parliament Martyn paid tribute to his mentor saying: 'Billy more than anyone taught me about truth and honesty in politics. I will make a solemn promise that I will follow in Billy's footsteps and fight against the renewal of Trident missiles.' Martyn emphasised that his vision for Scotland is to be without nuclear arms: 'It starts off being independent, it starts of being nuclear free, and I think the social democratic nature of our people will take it in the right direction. We will become much less divisive, much more equal.'

After working at the Bank of Scotland, Martyn was elected to West Lothian Council in the Scottish local elections in 1999 representing the Linlithgow ward and becoming a full-time councillor. Then, from 2007 to 2012, the SNP became the leaders of West Lothian Council and Martyn held the portfolio of Development and Transport on the Council Executive and served on over forty committees and outside bodies. After the Scottish local elections in 2012 the SNP found themselves in opposition in West Lothian and Martyn took on the posts of Spokesperson for Development and Transport and Group Whip.

While a councillor, Martyn was particularly involved in the Referendum campaign, which he described as 'two and a half years of gruelling hard work'. Despite being greatly disappointed at the result of the vote, Martyn noticed the huge difference between the start and end of the campaign: 'At the beginning, we were not expecting anything like the vote we got so we really pulled the vote up and I definitely see that as a success.' When asked if he thought that the success in the Referendum campaign led to the election of the 56 Martyn said: 'I don't think it led directly to the election of the 56, I think the process of the Referendum brought independence a lot closer because it broke the mould. Prior to six months before the Referendum during the campaign itself, there was a habitualness that people voted like tribal football supporters. Whatever the team was, that's what they came out and supported. It didn't matter what the policies were, they just voted that way. The latter stage of the Referendum changed all that forever. People started thinking, what do we actually want? The election of the 56 was a consequence of that fundamental change.' Martyn then spoke about the differences between his campaigns to be councillor and the campaign for Westminster, explaining that he had never seen such excitement before: 'it felt more like a carnival atmosphere than a campaign'.

Now in Westminster, Martyn is getting used to being a Westminster MP: 'Westminster is a fantastic tourist attraction, it is a remarkable building filled with heritage and lots of lovely and unique pieces of artwork but it is not a model office – it's certainly not how a parliament should be anyway. Everything you have to do takes so long and as well as that you're constantly on the hoof to get between places. My mother said at the start of the campaign: "Martyn, nobody in their right mind would want to go to Westminster!" and I think she's probably correct!'

This term Martyn has been chosen to sit on the select committee for administration, and in parliament his key focus will be helping 'people [to get] their fair share and representing people – being helpful to the less advantaged', though he will also 'fight as hard as I possibly can for every single constituent in this constituency. It doesn't matter how they voted in the Referendum, it doesn't matter how they voted in this election, I will fight tooth and nail for their interests.' One of Martyn's first acts as an MP was giving his £7000 MP pay rise to charitable causes in his constituency. As an avid campaigner for nuclear disarmament Martyn also vows to fight against nuclear arms: 'The single most appalling part of the Tory's Queen's Speech is the replacement of the trident nuclear system.'

Outside of politics Martyn enjoys reading and listening to music; 'When I'm reading it's mainly histories and biographies. In terms of music I particularly enjoy the folk scene although I'll listen to pretty much anything!'.

40. LISA CAMERON
EAST KILBRIDE, STRATHAVEN, AND LESMAHAGOW

Lisa was born in Glasgow but when she was five months old her family relocated to the blossoming new town of East Kilbride, where her mother had just started working as a secretary for Rolls Royce. Deciding it was the right time to move their family into Scotland's largest new town, the Camerons moved into the rapidly developing Westwood area. It was different compared to the cramped nature of Glasgow in the seventies.

From a young age Lisa showed academic potential, and although none of her family had gone to university before, it became an early ambition of hers. The first thought of university actually arose from the suggestion of her primary teacher: 'I remember in my report card it said that "Lisa could do well – she might even go to university". My family was made up at that comment.' While going to university was a conscious goal, Lisa never quite knew what she would study. In the end but still unsure, she chose to study English alongside a few other subjects. The hope was that throughout her first year at the University of Strathclyde she would be able to sample many different subjects before choosing to focus on one in later years. It didn't take long, however, for her to find that Psychology was a subject which fascinated her: by her final year she had dropped all her other subjects to focus on attaining a Bachelor's degree in Psychology.

After university Lisa described how she 'knew I wanted to become a clinical psychologist'. Her desire to become a clinical psychologist meant she would have to apply for a doctorate course but without field experience and a further degree it was unlikely she would be accepted. With that in mind Lisa decided to go back to university to study for a Masters in Psychology and Health at the University of Stirling. Afterwards, she worked as an assistant psychologist for a year at the Heartwood Hospital: 'It was a bit daunting at the time. They were closing [the hospital] down and it was a really old Victorian-style hospital. The patients had been there for years so it was like their home, but they were being moved out into the community and I was part of the re-location team.' Her role in helping to re-locate patients didn't make her – or her team – the favourite people in the hospital, but it was a job that convinced her even more of the need of psychological practices in both the medical profession and the NHS. After her year with Heartwood, she immediately applied for, and was accepted into, the University of Glasgow to study for a doctorate in Clinical Psychology.

After almost a decade of studying at different Scottish institutions, her graduation from the University of Glasgow in 1999 would be her last: she had finally gained the qualifications she required to enter the field of Clinical Psychology. Over the next fifteen years Lisa worked for the NHS in many hospitals across Scotland, but it was also with her entrance into the NHS that she got her first taste of politics, working as a trade union representative for Unite. This was, however, the politics of employment; it did not cross her mind that one day she might stand for parliament. To Lisa, politicians seemed to be a group of people 'sort of removed from everyday society', whereas by working for Unite, she was able to help and support her colleagues without having to deal with the complexities of partisan politics. But the Referendum on independence changed this.

The increase in debate over the NHS in Scotland spurred Lisa to get involved in both her local Yes Campaign and the NHS for Yes group: 'I was really concerned about the NHS in England and how that would impact on Scotland in terms of funding but also in terms of ideology.

When privatisation becomes the norm, then it is a slippery slope and one that is difficult for us to hold the tide back on.' Throughout the Referendum Lisa was an ever-present canvasser, hoping to persuade people of the positives of independence. But it wasn't to be. Her local area in South Lanarkshire delivered a resounding No vote on Referendum night.

The Referendum changed Lisa's views on politics: she no longer saw it as a role simply for career politicians but for people of all different experiences. It was mainly the actions of the now party Leader, Nicola Sturgeon, that caused the sea change in Lisa's opinion: 'I was so impressed by Nicola Sturgeon throughout the Referendum. I think she has that unique ability to reach out to people and make them believe in politics again.' It was that impression that convinced Lisa to put her name forward for the SNP, but in reality she hadn't expected to win the party's nomination. Instead it was simply to gain experience of the political process and to perhaps consider running again in the future. However, she was selected by the party to contest her home seat of East Kilbride, Strathaven, and Lesmahagow.

Two stalwarts of the SNP ran her campaign: former Glasgow councillor Duncan McLean and Ian McAllan. McAllan acted as her election agent, while McLean, having been East Kilbride's lead organiser during the referendum, led in organising the grassroots element of the campaign. For Lisa, entering into the campaign with only the experience of the Referendum, the support of both McAllan and McLean was invaluable to ensure that a major electoral operation was enacted.

On Election Day, the whole operation was run from what was once the base of YES East Kilbride. McLean took charge in overseeing the smooth running of East Kilbride's 'Get out the vote' operation, mobilising the small army of volunteers he had mustered for Lisa throughout the campaign. The day would go off without a hitch and come election night the atmosphere in East Kilbride's John Wright Sports Centre was electric for the SNP supporters. Canvassing had shown the party in a clear lead over Labour, and now there was a real chance to unseat Labour, who had held the seat since its inception back in 1974. The result was a repeat of the SNP's famous victory in 2011, when three female SNP candidates won the Labour party's South Lanarkshire heartland seats. Lisa, the first to be announced, overturned Labour's majority by gaining an incredible 16,527 majority of her own: 'I felt like I had won the lottery,' she said on hearing she'd won the election.

41. STEVEN PATERSON
STIRLING

Steven Paterson was born in Stirling Royal Infirmary in 1975. His father was an English teacher at St Modan's High School in Stirling and a local historian, and his mother was a nurse with the local health board. Steven said that his father has been one of the biggest influences on his life because 'he's a well-respected man who has fought for the causes he believes in, a lot of local causes – he very much believes in the village he's from, Cambusbarran. He has written books about the village and its history, trying to make sure things are written down for perpetuity so that things aren't forgotten, people aren't forgotten, he believes very passionately in that kind of cause. Also, I think that politically, he believes in fairness, he believes in social justice, which I very much take on. I look to him for it and he's someone to be inspired by, I think. A lot of people say to me that they were inspired by him as a teacher and I think that says a lot of things about him, too.'

Steven started his education at Cambusbarron Primary School before moving to Stirling High School, where had no aspirations of being a politician: 'I was extremely annoyed and irritated by the constant question of 'What do you want to be when you grow up?' when I was at school. I wanted to enjoy what I was doing at the time.

I never really had any ambitions in a political direction, although, looking back, I was a very political person at school when I think of it. I was involved and engaged in mock elections and I got a prize in Modern Studies – the only prize I got at high school. I just thoroughly enjoyed the whole concept and, when I was growing up, the news was always on at dinner time and things were talked about and news and current affairs was normal.' Steven went on to study Publishing at Robert Gordon University in Aberdeen. After university he went to Canada to travel, before coming back to Scotland and studying History and Politics at Stirling University where he graduated with honours.

Steven's interest in politics stems from his parents who 'were quite political people. My dad was involved in political campaigns in the 1980s, he was a schoolteacher and was a member of the Labour party and was involved in the campaigns then. Current affairs were a hot topic for discussion. I was always in favour of the SNP and, once I really had a chance to look at it, particularly looking at it from outside the country, and being asked the question 'does Scotland have its own government?' and the answer being 'no', it became clear it should have and it wasn't going to happen by itself. Political parties reflect views of the people so I got involved and here we are.'

Steven's involvement in politics began after his degree in Stirling, which had lead to the position of Media and Communications Manager for the SNP MSP Bruce Crawford in 2006. Talking about his career in politics before becoming an MP, Steven said: 'I'd been involved in many campaigns locally, in terms of election campaigns – Westminster elections, Scottish elections, and one or two local by-elections, the last of which we won, which is the first one we'd won locally in Stirling. That was the Borestone by-election of 2006. Scott Farmer became the only SNP councillor on the council. Around about that time we were looking for candidates for 2007 and it became a case of put up or shut up and I was quite prepared to put up, so I said I would be a candidate and I was and I won.' In January of 2013 Steven was appointed Deputy SNP group leader at Stirling council.

Steven went on to discuss the issues he faced while working as a councillor: 'When I look back now it is clear that the major disaffection with the Labour Party and the arrogance that that party had for

184

elections for power and for its entire performance was there, and it was growing. It reached its zenith, perhaps, this year, perhaps, because they [only] got one MP, but we're not quite there yet! I think you could definitely tell that people were sick and tired of the Labour Party who took it for granted that they would always win elections. I remember, in the Borestone by-election [...] the Labour candidate came up to me as I was putting a poster on a lamppost and he said "I congratulate you for your efforts but you know, son, this is a Labour ward". And then we won that election.'

Steven talked about the Scottish Referendum campaign: 'I thoroughly enjoyed it, until the polls closed and then it was not so good! Again, with six to eight months of time to look back on it, I think an interesting academic debate over the next few decades would be who won the Referendum because, whilst it [was clear] the No side had won the Referendum on the 19th of September, I don't think it's at all clear if that's the case now, and whether we're finished it yet – I don't think that we are. The fact that an unbelievable 56 out of 59 MPs are from the Scottish National Party – find me a western democracy where that's happened, where a party has won by that proportion. It is just incredible.'

In 2015, Steven was elected MP for Stirling with a 45.6% share of the vote taking the constituency away from Labour. Commenting on some of the worst Tory policies that he has experienced since his election as an MP, Steven said: 'There's an arrogance of a different kind with the Tories. This week in parliament they talked about English Votes for English Laws. Now, I have a great deal of sympathy for that argument, provided that it's alongside Scottish votes for Scottish laws, but the Tories don't see it that way. They want to have their cake and they want to eat their cake. When it comes to the Scotland Bill, first of all they officially consider it an England- and Wales-only bill, which is incredible – perhaps we'll give them the benefit of the doubt and that was a mistake by a civil servant, perhaps it was, however their one [Scottish] Tory MP is prepared to stand up and say that they'll listen to views – that's great, David, and then bring his 300 pals to vote down every single amendment the SNP brings up, bearing in mind we have 56 out of 59 MPs, is outrageous.'

Many of the 56 clearly express their dissatisfaction with the Westminster system, but Steven believes it can be put to use positively: 'Well, I'll never lose my belief that we're better governing ourselves here in Scotland. In terms of the way Westminster works, it has some archaic and confusing conventions. However, it's like any other parliament: it's got its rules, there are ways to make them work to your advantage if you understand them; I've tried to make quick work of getting to know exactly how it works. Every parliament has its own particular quirks – this one certainly does – but I'm enjoying getting into it. It does work, in a funny kind of way. It works best for the government but it can work for the opposition if you can find a way to exploit it. For example, Alistair Carmichael moved Standing Order 24, which forced a debate on English Votes for English Laws, which the Tories then had to walk away from because they didn't have the support of their own group. That was a way of exploiting a rule that's seldom used. Apparently Standing Order 24 usually fails because you have to have at least forty standing up to support it. When Carmichael moved it he knew he had our support and we're 56, and he had Labour support and he had the Ulster Unionists and he had the SDLP, so half the chamber stood up and the speaker had to just say, "Clearly there is support for this and we'll [hold an] emergency debate tomorrow". You can use an obscure rule, one that's not used often, and you can use it well to embarrass the government. And we did.'

In his spare time Steven keeps fit by going on runs, going to the gym, and doing karate. He also enjoys watching the Scotland football team play, home or away: 'It might be a lot more challenging to be at all the games but I'll try to get to as many as I can. It looks like I'll manage to get to Georgia this year, which is good. It might be a bit more challenging to get to a home game with Germany because of parliamentary commitments but we'll just see about that.' When Steven was asked about his vision for a future Scotland, his answer was simple: 'I want a Scotland where we get the government we vote for every time, not once in a blue moon.'

42. PETE WISHART
PERTH AND NORTH PERTHSHIRE

Pete Wishart is not only a successful politician having worked for the SNP in Tayside since 2001, but he's also a successful musician having been a member of Runrig for fifteen years. Pete's interest in both music and politics started at an early age in his childhood home of Dunfermline. Pete was never very academic at school and was much more involved with music: 'I remember before going on tour with my first band being in support of The Skids the week that I had my O grades, which didn't go down particularly well in my household with my mother and father. That was when punk rock music had come along in the late 1970s, that's what consumed all my attention. I did manage to scrape enough qualifications to get into college and I studied Community Education at Moray House where the whole course was run by Marxists who were very keen to give us a proper and detailed political background.'

While studying at Moray House Pete found himself involved in his first major musical project: 'I had just done one year at Moray House and I was recruited to join the first line up of Big Country. Coming from Dunfermline I was good friends with Stuart Adamson and my first band had toured with The Skids so I became very friendly with

Stuart and I was asked to help set up [...] Big Country so I left college thinking that it was the beginning of a long and productive music career and, of course, it all ended within a year. Thankfully I retained my college place and was able to go back after that year. After going back to college I tried to get a job as a community worker and I worked in children's homes for six months until I was eventually recruited to join Runrig as they'd heard of a guy who'd played keyboard for Big Country, so I was effectively headhunted by them because they were massive Big Country fans. So from about 1985, from then I was in the band right up until my election in 2001.'

Pete's time in Runrig turned out to be a good precursor to going in to politics: 'There was a huge interest in politics in Runrig, particularly around the Gaelic language. One of the things I'm most proud about is that we introduced Gaelic to a new young generation of people who then saw its worth. We felt that we had control of a lost part of our history, which had almost been killed off by a number of UK or British interests. While we were trying to re-engender some interest in the language we encountered other political issues, things like land reform and the condition of the Highlands. We were naturally drawn into other political interests and issues, and with the time of the Scottish Parliament coming, Runrig practically became the soundtrack to it. We did lots of events and gigs. We did Stirling Castle in 1992 and I'll never forget, when all the big Scottish bands, Deacon Blue and Wet Wet Wet were all there playing for the cause of the Scottish Parliament. For most rock bands on tour, the back of the tour bus would be about sex drugs and rock and roll, with Runrig it was a debate about Scotland's constitutional questions.'

Pete's political upbringing stems from his home life: 'I have a particularly political background; as my grandfather was a leader in the miners' union in Kelty in west Fife which meant there was always political discussion and debate in the household. My grandad always told me when we were watching early TV to look out for Tony Benn and Eric Heffer, and he was interested in what they had to contribute to the political debate that was going around at that point.'

Pete was not always a member of the SNP: 'I was in the Labour Party – because of my background it was a natural progression – for most of the early 1980s, I was student union president, I was president of Moray House for a year and that was on the back of being a Labour party activist. I was in the party until Kinnock started the whole modernisation process and I, like quite a lot of people of my generation and background, slowly disentangled myself from the party, spent a few years looking around the market place, not fully committed to the SNP. I finally joined up in the early 1990s.'

Pete was first elected to the House of Commons, taking John Swinney's old seat of Tayside North. Pete has had several positions since arriving at Westminster including serving as the SNP's Chief Whip, through which he has pressed the government for greater representation on committees for minority parties. One of Pete's other achievements while at Westminster is forming a band: 'As soon as I was elected I saw there wasn't a cross-party music group so I hastily put that together – MP4 – the world's only parliamentary rock band. We've reached the steady height of competence after 10 years together! It's cross-party and like most MPs from different parties who do things together, it's probably the only time you don't discuss politics as there's no point.'

Pete said that he really enjoyed the Scottish Independence Referendum campaign in 2014: 'it was just fascinating and brilliant and I found it totally rejuvenating.' He spoke about the lasting effects of the campaign in his constituency: 'I remember convening meetings in Perthshire with John Swinney that still had hundreds turning up. I think in that sense it was unfinished business. People were waiting for the next stage to ensure our nation gained independence and there was determination and refocus on how it could continue to be relevant, and this was helped by the vast membership to the SNP which happened right after the election. I was one of the few Scottish members of parliament that didn't have many concerns about my re-election and I got the feeling that if people were going to be losing seats in Scotland it wouldn't be the SNP. Putting together the anti-austerity case across the United Kingdom was something that during my election campaign I was able to work on and shape up a little.'

Pete has seen a big change in Westminster since the 56 were elected: 'in the past because there were only six of us it was a scattered affair

– I had to look after four departments, and was also the Chief Whip. All of us had massive and multiple tasks that we had to perform, and to give credit to my colleagues, it was something the small group did exceptionally well. To go back down [to Westminster] with the 56 and to have all these talented colleagues who have expertise and skills was just great, so I could concentrate on one or two issues that are now exclusively my responsibility.'

Pete's ultimate goal is 'to see my nation independent and I think that's certainly going to happen. I think that the last Referendum experience gave us a sense and an idea about the way in which we want to see a future Scotland develop and emerge and I think we can start to reimagine and reconstruct the vision we want to achieve; we've got quite a lot to build on now. Community values build on the common weal we have in this nation. One of the things that disappoints me a little [and] that we didn't get across is that we've got to contribute internationally as a nation: the solid historical and cultural values we have, what we can bring, and the profound contribution we'll be able to make as an independent nation. We are almost unique in the features we have as a society and nation to make that kind of impression.'

Pete finished by stating how influential Stuart Adamson had been on his career, and how the opportunities he presented led to where he is today: 'For me the thing that changed my life from being an ordinary kid at school, that gave such a tangible impression for me to realise my potential, was meeting Stuart Adamson. If Stuart hadn't come along with Big Country, all the rest of the stuff wouldn't have happened. My move into politics wouldn't have been as seamless without Runrig. Music was always my first love although politics is my main love. This is someone I am very proud to have called a close personal friend and had he not asked me to join Big Country when I was eighteen years old quite a lot of this wonderful experience I've had wouldn't have been realised so of all the people who've made a difference the one who came along first with an opportunity was Stuart Adamson.'

43. TASMINA AHMED-SHEIKH
OCHIL AND SOUTH PERTHSHIRE

Tasmina Ahmed-Sheikh is a successful businesswoman, actress, lawyer and now MP, winning the seat of Ochil and South Perthshire with 46% of the vote. Tasmina was born in Chelsea in 1970, where she lived for the first five years of her life before her family moved to Edinburgh. Tasmina went to primary school in Corstorphine then moved to the Mary Erskine School for a year, before attending the local state school, Craigmount High, then undertaking fifth and sixth year at George Heriot's School. Tasmina noted the lack of racial diversity in these Scottish schools: 'I'm mixed race; my father is Pakistani and my mother is half-Welsh and half-Czech, and I was the only child in primary school, and most of secondary school, of mixed race, and this had its challenges. I was one of the first mixed race kids, it's now the norm, but it wasn't at the time.'

Tasmina stayed in Edinburgh to attend university and she studied English Literature, Economics, and International Law. Finishing her degree at the age of twenty, she married that same year. She then moved to Pakistan for a while, undertaking some modelling work while being cast for, then starring in, the television series *Des Parades*. Tasmina explained the reasons for her return to Scotland: 'Once I had done that for a couple of years I wanted to come back and complete my education, so I went to Strathclyde [University] and did the accelerated two-year graduate degree for Law. I was pregnant with my first child while sitting the final exams for that and actually gave birth a couple of days after my graduation, so I'm a woman who has worked throughout her life and has had children while I've been going along.' After completing her degree Tasmina became a lawyer, but she has also been involved in television programmes in Scotland.

Tasmina's political life started early when she helped her father with his campaigns: 'My politics stemmed from the same situation as my children currently find themselves in, which is living in a political household. My father came from Pakistan and joined the Conservative Party and became a regional councillor in the 1980s for Edinburgh Central. He was the first regional councillor in the whole of Scotland of Asian origin. I remember as a young girl spending a lot of time with my sister and my mum delivering leaflets and canvassing for him.'

Tasmina initially joined the Conservative party and was a member of the Young Conservatives during her time in Edinburgh. She stood as the party's candidate in Glasgow Govan in the 1999 Scottish Parliament election. I asked Tasmina what drew her from the Conservatives to the SNP party, she said that a key moment for her was when she 'moved from canvassing the leafy suburbs of Edinburgh having a fairly good protected environment to canvassing on the streets of Govan. I found out what life was really like for the people on the ground giving me a first-hand insight into what was really happening to the people of Scotland as an adult, and at that point as a mum. It completely changed my view on life from what I thought we needed to progress and it was therefore after that election that I didn't think the current UK framework was helping people and so I joined the SNP. It is worthy of note that I was number two on the Conservative Party list and had I stayed, I would have been elected many, many years before I got elected as an SNP parliamentarian.'

Tasmina became involved in the 2014 Referendum, where she was asked to be on the board of Yes Scotland. Subsequently, she was actively involved in a number of different independence organisations due to her breadth of expertise: 'I was actively involved in Scottish

Students for Independence, Lawyers for Yes, Women for Independence and Businesses for Scotland as I have a number of different areas of experience. It was a campaign which brought together voices from across Scotland like never before, and I think [that] for the first time members of the Asian community, women, and businesses were given spaces to air their views and say what Scotland meant for them. The biggest challenge post-Referendum was to ensure that we stayed a very engaged population and that has succeeded, as I saw in my General Election campaign. The people I spoke to knew about different areas, whether it was the economy or immigration, and the questions were not basic, they were detailed, well thought out questions about 'What does this mean for me? Why is our economy controlled by Westminster, why do we have foodbanks?' These challenging questions on the doorstop suggested that people read up during the Referendum and continued to read about politics and engage via social media too, which allowed them to ask important questions to politicians that were knocking on the doors. Something that has been noted by people down south in the House of Commons is that Scotland has a very engaged population, and many politicians from different political parties often say that they wished it was the same where they were canvassing.'

Tasmina has both historical and political inspirations: 'I would probably say from a historical perspective the founder of Pakistan Muhammad Ali Jinnah and Gandhi [are inspirations]. I think from the deal they had to come to in those very difficult times to get peace we can learn lessons about the pen being much mightier than the sword. I would say in modern day life absolutely Nicola Sturgeon, because she has encouraged me [to] no end in the European elections when I first stood for the SNP and encouraged me as an individual but also as a woman and as a member of the Asian community. In the face of many issues that women can face including misogyny, sexism, and in my case racism and some prejudice, Nicola encourages us to keep going and we know she is there to support us and that's huge. The biggest challenge for successful women is to make sure they are bringing up all those women behind them that look up to them, which is something Nicola has done and continues to do.'

As an MP, Tasmina has a number of main focuses as both SNP

Trade and Investment Spokesperson and Deputy Shadow Leader of the House. As Deputy Shadow Leader, debates have been a focus for her, with the implementation of a debate on trident within in the first week. At the moment as Trade and Investment spokesperson, one of Tasmina's focuses is the Transatlantic Trade and Investment Partnership: 'There seems to be a lot of questions that are unanswered and we're not prepared to let the government tell us that public services are going to be protected unless we see that in writing.' She is also concerned with Scotland maximising its potential in foreign markets 'in terms of inward investment as well as our ability to export. The export figures [...] in the quorum court show there is a long way to go, so I'm working with the Scottish Government to make sure our businesses can succeed at home and abroad.'

Tasmina then talked about how she spends any time away from politics: 'I have four children who quite rightly occupy the majority of my spare time. I'm also involved with community work with the Scottish Asian community and the business community. I'm involved in a number of charities, one being Scottish Women in Sport, which I'm a trustee at, and I work with Judy Murray, Katherine Grainger, and a number of women to ensure that our young people of school age are taking up sporting opportunities given to them and that we get media coverage. That is an issue that faces women in sport – that we don't get the same coverage as men do – and also to make sure that sponsorship deals are available for women too.' Furthermore, Tasmina is the only Asian woman to ever be elected to any parliament from Scotland, and she is also a trustee for W1 as she explained: 'W1 is an organisation for multiethnic women and I'm a trustee for Scottish Asian Women, which, again, looks to empower Asian women living in Scotland and encourage them to become part of civil society.'

Tasmina spoke of what she hopes to see for Scotland in the future: 'What I would like to see is an independent Scotland, I would like my children to grow up in an independent Scotland. That is, however, if it is the will of the Scottish people. We will continue to work with that vision but also with the will of the people, and if they want us to work within the current UK constitutional framework that is what we will do and we will make sure that Scotland is well and truly on the map.'

44. DOUGLAS CHAPMAN
DUNFERMLINE AND WEST FIFE

Douglas Chapman has lived in his constituency for twenty-three years and 2015 saw him deliver his fourth General Election campaign. In the 2015 General Election he took a massive 50.3% of the overall vote with a 39.6% swing from his Labour predecessor Thomas Docherty. Douglas was born in Edinburgh in 1955 before moving to West Lothian and growing up in Livingstone and East Calder. Douglas went to school at West Calder High and afterwards went straight into the world of work which he now regrets: 'In those days the expectations for people going to University was definitely not as high and my parents never encouraged me to do anything like that, but looking back now, that is something I should have pursued. It was a different time though. I'm a bit jealous of my own children, and my daughter's going to one which will put her in good stead.'

Although Douglas was always engaged in politics he didn't get actively involved until he became a volunteer for a local election in Rosyth in 1990. His interest came from his family: 'My father was quite political, and I think my interest stemmed from that usual Scottish habit of shouting at the TV when there're things that people say that you disagree with. He was involved in a trade union as well which

I think gave him a bit of an edge on the family discussions around the table.' However, Douglas was not always involved with the SNP: 'I remember being a young sixteen-year-old going along to a Labour meeting though I lasted virtually one meeting. I found it depressing that they always argued amongst themselves, and for a sixteen-year-old you have strong ideals and you want them to be listened to and it wasn't the forum for me. The first couple of times I voted it was for Labour – it was always a Labour area I was brought up in. I think it was the failed first Referendum that changed my mind about whether to vote Labour or SNP which I've been ever since.'

As well as causing his switch to the SNP, Douglas's active part in politics was triggered by the first devolution Referendum: 'The thing that really changed it for a lot of people in my generation was the way that the first Referendum on devolution was hijacked with the introduction of the 40% rule, where even the people that were dead technically had a vote. That really angered me, but I think I was always very pro-Scotland and I didn't see how Scottish interests were best served though Westminster. Yet, here I am today, trying to serve Scottish interests as best I can through Westminster.'

Douglas went on from discussing the first Referendum on devolution to talking about how he easily came to terms with the No result from the 2014 Referendum: 'I was one of the campaign managers when the Scottish Government was elected on a minority SNP basis. I've been around the party for a long time. You begin to factor in levels of disappointment sometimes. I wasn't too upset, actually, after the Referendum, and the rise in the party membership really compensated [for] some of the bad feeling on the 19th. Now, for the people of Scotland to put their faith in us is really humbling as well.'

'The 2014 Referendum has definitely brought independence closer. I wouldn't like to put a date on it but I think we are moving towards independence faster than we maybe think. I think that whoever chooses the date for the next Referendum will have to make sure it is absolutely spot-on and in the bag before we start, as we cannot afford to have another Referendum where we lose by 1 or 2%, we have to win it. The risk of going into Referendum and losing is unthinkable.'

Having stood for elections in the past, when asked whether he went into the 2015 election knowing that it would be the year when he would be successful, Douglas replied: 'I did feel this time we had a real opportunity, especially after the Referendum, to make big in-roads and have a really strong voice at Westminster and I felt that my time had come in some respects and I feel like I can be that voice for the constituency. I wanted to represent the constituency I live in and didn't seek nominations elsewhere as I wanted to do the best for the people that I've lived for twenty years with.'

Now down in Westminster, Douglas explained what he wanted to achieve personally while in parliament: 'I see this as a huge opportunity to expand my experience; maybe it's come a bit later in my life than I might have hoped but there are good opportunities here. I've just joined, for example, the cross-party group on Japan. Japan is a country that most people find fascinating but don't really understand the life, culture, and so on. I would like to spend the next five years learning about Japan and how it could affect Scotland – what kind of relationship we could have with a country that doesn't necessarily share our culture.'

He then went on to speak about what he will particularly focus on: 'I think we need to challenge the sense of right the Conservatives have as the government at every opportunity. Whether that's on High Speed Rail or the economy, where there are these twelve billion pounds of benefit cuts, we will form a strong opposition to these things. Not because they are Tories or Tory policy, but because these might not be the right things for Scotland or the rest of the UK.'

After that Douglas discussed Westminster traditions: 'I think it's easy to see why Britain lost its Empire. The conventions have been developed over a long period of time and I think it's part of our job here to jab Westminster into the next century: this century. Given that this is at the very heart of the establishment, things will take a while to shift. We need to be patient and do things in a way that wins support across other parties as well. The House Authorities who run the whole thing do well to not make the whole thing seem so antiquated and it feeds into the agenda of the Commons being out of touch and politicians being out of touch with the modern world.' Douglas is steered by a vision of a fairer Scotland because he's 'always' wanted 'Scotland to be the most successful country it can be. We have huge issues with the health of the nation and levels of poverty, especially amongst young children. These have been the driving factors for me throughout my whole political career. If we can create the kind of country where everyone has a fair chance then that is the overall goal.'

Politics aside, Douglas is a loyal fan of Hibs and his family all have season tickets to Easter Road: 'We go along as often as we can, every home game this season.' Douglas, a father of two, also highlighted how important family life is to him: 'I like to spend time with my family – my wife has a lot of relatives so I've been trying to spend time with them, enjoy each other's company, and relaxing. My kids are into swimming and there're quite a few things we have to do to make sure they get their training every week. Family life, at the moment, is really, really valuable, and I'm loving being back in Scotland for short periods of time as you focus much more in the time you do have.'

Douglas's son is also a source of inspiration: 'I think [the] one person that really inspires me is my son. Andrew is thirteen years old and he has Down's Syndrome. There is nothing in his life that he cannot do. When I'm faced with things like taking the oath or doing my first maiden speech I think, 'Well, if he can do things in his life that are a great challenge to him, I've got it fairly easy.' It's a little bit of a reminder from time to time that even though everyone has their own difficulties and problems they are there to be overcome. In my own little way as well I hope to be an inspiration to others who will think 'If he can do it, so can I'.'

45. STEPHEN GETHINS
NORTH EAST FIFE

Despite being a 'proper east coaster' Stephen Gethins's outlook has always been far more international than local. He grew up in Perth in the late seventies and early eighties with a curiosity for the unknown and a desire to be an explorer. Initially his dream was to follow in the footsteps of his original hero Indiana Jones and become an archaeologist, but this dream did not last long. It was overtaken by a much deeper passion for politics and independence. Stephen's dad, a teacher, was heavily involved in the trade union movement, but Stephen's real encouragement in politics came from his grandparents who were long-standing believers in independence. As Stephen's belief and determination for independence grew, the SNP was the only political party he could contemplate joining.

'I felt very at home politically in the SNP,' he says having joined the party at seventeen while still in high school. 'What always drove me was the international outlook. I always thought the real isolation was the Union, and it frustrated me that you had to deal with the rest of the world through the prism of London. The idea of Scotland re-joining the family of nations in Europe was also what really drove me.'

His political decision to support the SNP didn't seem prosperous at the time: both the MP for Perth and the MP for North of Perth belonged to the Scottish Conservative Party and Unionist Party. However, his first taste of political victory wouldn't be long awaited: having joined the party in 1993 he thrust himself into the 1995 Perth and Kinross by-election. At the time it seemed like it would be a victory for the Labour Party and their young rising star, Douglas Alexander, who would later become the Shadow Foreign Secretary. In the end the SNP's Roseanna Cunningham secured the seat, giving Stephen his first real political experience. This did not, however, spur him onto the idea of an early political career: 'Going into elected politics in my early twenties wasn't the right thing for me.'

After graduating from the University of Dundee with a degree in Law, Stephen decided to combine his childhood passions of exploration and politics. Leaving Scotland he worked for the NGO Saferworld, as Stephen explained: 'I [...] worked in the former Soviet Union for eight years. Working in Georgia, Armenia and Azerbaijan was fascinating. You got a really good insight into life in those countries, and I realised just how lucky we are in Scotland to have a sensible debate and live in a society that is largely at peace with itself.'

Much of Stephen's time was spent in the internationally unrecognised states of South Ossetia and Abkhazia, working on inter-ethnic conflict and post-Soviet reconstruction. As one of the world's most ethnically diverse and politically complicated regions, the arena of Scottish nationalism would seem very distant. Yet as Stephen recalled: 'the Caucasians have a huge soft spot for Scotland. The Caucasus is part of the ancient kingdom of Scythia in which the Treaty of Arbroath refers to the Scots as being "we of Scythian origin", and Caucasians loved that. We thought we were brothers and sisters. Scotland stretches from one end of the farthest regions of Europe to the other. Even Burns was translated into South Ossetian.'

Stephen's far-eastern adventure eventually ended following an opportunity to work within the European Union. As an admirer of the late Scottish MEP Dr Allan Macartney, Europe had always held a special place in his heart. Having had a year abroad in Antwerp while at university, Belgium had always held nostalgic feeling for Stephen, and his new position was as Policy Advisor to the Committee of Regions, the European Union's gathering place for European local government officials.

Eventually Stephen returned to Scotland to work for the newly elected nationalist government in 2009, as a special advisor to many of the government ministers. The chance to work alongside the great figures of the SNP was too much for Stephen to turn down: 'It was a real privilege to work so closely with Alex Salmond as First Minister, and to get an insight into how government and the civil service works.' His role within the SNP Government would regularly fluctuate, from one month working with John Swinney on budget and financial matters, to the next working alongside Richard Lochhead on rural affairs policy. In many ways, Stephen acted as a jack-of-all-trades within the administration: he provided calm perspective and gained the reputation as a rising star within the party.

When leaving his position as a Special Advisor to the Government, Stephen didn't immediately seek election. Instead, returning to his childhood desire to see the world, he headed to the African continent. However, much like when in the Caucasus, he wasn't as far away from Scotland as he thought: 'I went to do a lot of work in Namibia. What I didn't realise, was that SWAPO (the political party in charge of Namibia since its independence) have a huge soft spot for Scotland. The first democratically established newspaper in Namibia was established in Glasgow and it is still on the go.'

Stephen finally sought the chance to be elected in 2014, when he was chosen to be the SNP's fourth candidate in the European elections. The likelihood of the SNP achieving three seats at the election was already a difficult task, nevermind winning a fourth, and Stephen's first foray into electoral politics didn't end as successfully as he had hoped. However 2014 was not a complete disaster for Stephen, and while his loss in the European Elections coincided with the loss of the Independence Referendum, he witnessed the birth of his first child, a baby daughter.

Stephen, true to his east coast roots, ran for the seat of North East Fife, a Liberal Democrat stronghold for over a quarter of a century. With a young family, the idea of working across the globe no longer had the same appeal for Stephen. But his interest in international affairs was still a huge focus, and the opportunity arose to run for the Parliament in Westminster: 'I have been focused on international affairs my whole life and this is where it is at. I don't happen to like it – I would rather not [...] commute down here every week. But this is where a lot of policies that will continue to govern us will be made.' In many ways, his victory reflects his journey across many parts of the world when, somehow, he always found a connection to Scotland. As he was sworn into the Commons he wore the tartan tie of the Scottish Parliament in a small act of defiance – a nod to the 'senior institution' he said, without a hint of sarcasm. His parting comments were: 'We are here [in Westminster] to settle up, not settle down.'

46. PETER GRANT
GLENROTHES

Peter Grant was born in 1961 in Coatbridge into a staunchly Labour supporting family. He recalls that his father would tell him: 'The Tories are only for rich people, the Liberals are watered down Tories, and the SNP are tartan Tories. That's why you vote Labour.' Politics were important to his father, and his fervour for Labour transferred to Peter for a short time. As a youngster Peter was more interested in music than he was in politics: he learnt to play the piano and there was always a part of him that dreamed of what it might be like to become a professional musician. Unlike many of his school friends, Peter went on to study Physics at the University of Glasgow in 1977 before going on to gain a further qualification in teaching. He taught Physics at schools in Ayrshire and Fife including spending a short time working in the Civil Service at the Health and Safety Executive (HSE) during the time of Margaret Thatcher's government. It was around then that he started to reconsider the political notions that his father had taught him growing up. '[Working in the days of Margaret Thatcher] persuaded many people about the benefits of having a government of our own,' he joked.

Once he left the civil service and had began re-training as an accountant he settled in Glenrothes, and decided that the SNP now truly represented him in a way that Labour had failed to for a long time. Yet it wasn't until 1987 that he decided it was time to track down a party official and join its ranks: 'It was difficult to track anybody down before the days of the internet. Eventually a friend put me in touch with an SNP contact called Patricia Marwick, and I duly phoned her.' In the late 1980s the SNP's membership cards were simply just cardboard so they had to be signed manually by a branch officer. The branch officer in Fife was Patricia Marwick who signed his card as 'Tricia Marwick', as Peter remarked: 'The first SNP membership card I ever had was signed by Holyrood's future Presiding Officer.'

After leaving the civil service, Peter started working multiple local government positions and then later with the NHS in finance, but he mainly focused on his passion for the SNP. In 1992, only five years after joining the party, he stood for election and won his local council seat for the SNP in a time where Labour still completely dominated local government in Scotland. By the 2007 elections, however, with the SNP under Peter's leadership, they more than doubled their number of council seats, overtaking the Liberal Democrats for the first time ever in the number of seats and coming behind Labour by just one. Following the election Peter would form an SNP-Lib Dem coalition on Fife council and become the council's first ever non-Labour leader since the local government restructuring in 1995.

Soon after becoming Fife's council leader, a by-election occurred in Glenrothes following the death of the Labour MP John MacDougall. It was an exciting time for the party: the SNP had been in Government for over a year at Holyrood and had just won the Glasgow East by-election. Many people thought that the SNP would be the favourite to win the seat and Peter was chosen to contest the election. However, the Labour Party managed to hold on, despite a 5% swing towards the SNP. The result was disappointing for Peter, but by putting a lot of effort into attempting to win the seat and having delivered a strong performance, the party was in its best ever position historically.

By the time of the 2012 council elections, despite an increase in the SNP's total number of seats on the council, the collapse of the Liberal Democrats was to the Labour Party's benefit. Indeed, they finished the election significantly ahead of the SNP in terms of the number of seats won, and formed a minority administration in Fife after the election. This saw Peter lose his position as council leader: instead he became the new leader of the opposition.

The blow of losing control of the council was softened by the fact that there was to be a Referendum on independence, and by 2013, Peter had left his part-time job as a finance manager in order to spend time organising and campaigning for a Yes vote in Fife. The result in Fife was a microcosm of the rest of Scotland: it voted to remain part of the United Kingdom. Having seen the SNP at the lows of Fife council in the early 1990s with only nine councillors against a Labour majority, Peter was convinced that while the Referendum was a No vote it wasn't the end for the SNP. Convinced that the party needed a strong candidate in Glenrothes if it was to win the seat, Peter put himself forward hoping to be successful a second time around: 'I remember telling branch meetings that we had to treat Glenrothes as a marginal even though we were fighting a 16,000-plus majority,' he recalled.

He was selected by the party and became sure that the seat could be won, but he knew this would require a huge effort: 'The way the campaign team pulled itself together was like nothing I've ever seen before. We really did have people from all walks of life, all wanting to be heard.'

The campaign was an intense period, with many polls suggesting that Labour MPs with huge majorities could fall. Momentum for the SNP was seen from early on, but it soon rose exponentially when former Labour councillors – including the former leader of Kirkcaldy district council – publically announced that they would be backing the SNP over Labour in the election. The momentum culminated in a spontaneous mass rally three days before the election, when Nicola Sturgeon arrived in Glenrothes to campaign on behalf of Peter Grant. On election night the campaign received a huge response from people who said that they would be backing the SNP and Peter. It seemed very likely that the party would win the seat. The final result was a shock, even to the SNP activists at the count: the party received a 35% swing – at that time a record swing for a General Election – only to later be beaten by Anne McLaughlin who gained almost 60% of the overall vote.

In his maiden speech to the House of Commons Peter recalled the events of the Referendum and gave a defiant statement on the future of the SNP: 'The reason the SNP benches are usually so packed is that one of the four equal partner nations in this Union has once again dared to hope and dared to believe in a better future. 'Project Fear' may have won the day in 2014. I am proud to stand here in 2015 as a representative of 'Project Hope', and Project Hope will prevail.'

47. ROGER MULLIN
KIRKCALDY AND COWDENBEATH

Roger Mullin is the SNP MP for the safest Labour seat in Scotland: Kircaldy and Cowdenbeath. Roger won the seat formerly held by Gordon Brown with an impressive 52% of the vote. Roger was born in Maybole and was educated at Carrick Academy, the same school as Marion Fellows, another member of the 56. Much to the bemusement of his parents, Roger was interested in politics from an early age and often made political statements unconsciously: 'In the mid-1950s the Queen was coming to visit Maybole and my mum and dad had a wee bakers business next to the town hall in Ayrshire. At the same time as a wee boy I was due to go into the hospital to have my tonsils and adenoids removed and I always remember my mum saying to me "the Queen's coming when you should be in the hospital in your operation so we can get the operation changed so you can see the Queen' and I apparently answered: "I would rather have my tonsils and adenoids out." I am told the reason I was particularly keen to have them out [rather] than see the Queen was because I had been promised a new football!'

Before going to university, Roger had already begun a career. While his brother and sister had gone to university directly from school, and although he had the qualifications that would have allowed him immediate entry, he decided to rebel and secured a job as a trainee electronic craftsman. He worked in this job for four years before becoming a designer for IBM: 'I really hated working at IBM so eventually I decided to give it up. At this time I was married to Barbara and she said, "give up this job, sell up the house, and go to university". So I then went in my twenties to Edinburgh University and studied Sociology and Politics but [I specialised] in the sociology aspects and I stayed on for a couple of years to do research after graduating.'

'After university I was drinking in Sandy Bells bar one day, and I was eighteen months into what was supposedly going to be a PhD and by this stage Barbara and I had two young children and I felt a bit bad about still being a student. By chance I met this chap in the bar who was from the West Lothian College and they were desperately trying to recruit somebody to be a lecturer in industrial sociology so I applied over the bar, was subsequently sent some papers, and in an extremely short space of time was given a job. I did get a number of publications out of the research that I'd done for my PhD, I helped write a book called *Multi-Party Britain* and I wrote a chapter in a book called *The Referendum Experience*, so the year and a half I'd spent doing research wasn't a complete waste of time.'

Roger decided to join the SNP as a teenager and he can recall three main reasons – connected to his family – that he joined the party: 'As a wee boy, my dad, after working down the mines and nearly being killed, joined the Territorial Army between the First and Second World Wars. He entered the Second World War and, very surprisingly for a working-class lad who had not gone to private school or anything, became a captain. He was serving at the end of the war in India and got the Burma Star Award for being a part of the Burma campaign. He always told me about how at the end of his time in India many senior officers – majors, colonels and the like, would all come to him to get him to fill out their forms to apply for different parts of the diplomatic service because he was brighter than them. He said to me, "I, of course, could not apply for anything because I didn't go to a private school". As a wee boy I was annoyed by what I subsequently knew was the class system so I became aggrieved particularly with my dad's pride in never getting an opportunity under the British Government.'

'The connection with my mother is that my Christian name, Roger, comes from my mother's side of the family with Roger as a surname. My ancestor was a man called Hugh Roger who was Robert Burns' teacher and my mother always used to sing Scots songs to me in bed at night, so I suppose you can say that Scottish cultural links would be from my mother's side. Then from my older brother who was eight years older than me and was very bright at school, did a double honours Masters in Physics at Glasgow University, [and] never, so far as we know, ever thought about going overseas, but [he] found he had to when he couldn't get a job in the UK. The only people who offered him a job was the Atomic Energy of Canada so he had to emigrate [...] I thought that this was absolutely ridiculous; somebody I thought to be tremendously bright and able couldn't get a job in his own country. I think these were the kind of influences that meant when I heard about this thing called the Scottish National Party from somebody else at school, I thought it sounded like the thing for me so I joined when I think I would've been about seventeen.'

Roger's father served not just as a reason for him to join the SNP: 'The person who inspired me more than anyone else is my father. I've never met any couple more caring about other people than my parents. When I was in the early stages of my marriage, they lived in a council house in Maybole and somewhere else in the town a house had had a fire and an elderly couple had been burned out of their home and would probably be rehoused in not very good circumstances. My parents, having never met them before, asked them to come and live in their house. They would do things like that, never trying to make a big deal of things but they were very caring about the community. My dad always had this mantra, he said that everybody in this world is good at something. In that sense, he not only cared, but admired the potential of people and would have wanted to see everybody having the opportunity to flourish.'

During the Referendum campaign in 2014, Roger really wanted to find out what the campaign was like in different places so he travelled around: 'I did some work with [the] Margo Mobile [campaign]. I was out in Glasgow doing canvassing. I was out in Perthshire. I tried to do quite a lot of social media and the like. I wasn't playing a leading role, though. I was keen to do anything I could to get the Yes vote. I was tremendously impressed by the new generation of people getting involved and look forward to them taking it forward, but I wasn't a leading light in that way.'

Roger's career within the SNP has seen him be Vice-Convenor of the Party as well as an unsuccessful candidate in both the Paisley North by-election in 1990 and in the Paisley North General Election in 1992. He fought three other elections unsuccessfully for the SNP. When asked how he thought people's attitudes to the SNP had changed, he said: 'The thing that I had always hoped, and which has proven absolutely correct, is that a lot of people who were scared of the SNP, who thought that only two parties ever rule and nobody else could do it, I thought if we could ever demonstrate that actually there were a lot of able people who could manage things at least as well that would be a big turning point for us, so I think our first minority government was when things started to shift.'

As an MP in a seat once thought to be impenetrable because it was previously a Labour strong-hold, when asked what his main focuses are in Westminster he said: 'Three things in different areas: one is, having been a social scientist and studied behaviours, I am highly conscious about the great value of having effective binding and teamwork in the group. One thing I would say I would be able to do is make sure there are really strong bonds in the group. The second thing is I was not expecting to get asked to fulfill any particularly significant position so it came a bit out of the blue when I was asked if I would be a treasury Spokesperson. So long as I'm in the position I want to make as big an impact as I can. The third thing is I've done a lot of work overseas in the past. I've done twenty-seven assignments, half of them for the United Nations agencies, I've been in some troubled spots and, to my surprise I was confirmed as the chairman of the all-party parliamentary group that looks at land mines and unexploded weapons that are a danger to children and civilians throughout the world. I hope to make a difference there.'

Roger finished by outlining his long-term vision outside of the Westminster framework: 'I want Scotland to become the kind of country that the people of Scotland want it to become. My kind of Scotland is very outward-looking, I would want it to be one where it is still valued for development and entrepreneurial activity, it would be sustainable, but then to understand that it needs to be matched by a moral dimension.'

48. HANNAH BARDELL
LIVINGSTON

Hannah Bardell, the new SNP MP for Livingston, was born in 1984 at Bangour Hospital. Bangour had been a war hospital in World War Two and despite the fact that this was forty years before, Hannah always appreciated the idea that she was born in a war hospital because it let her imagination run wild as a child. In her youth she developed a passion for football, often playing with her younger brother and grandfather: 'I was a bit of a tomboy. My brother and I [...] were always kicking the ball around out back.' Her mother, who had worked as a university lecturer throughout her childhood, had been the first in her family to go to university. Hannah grew up hoping to emulate what her mother had achieved: 'I felt it was an important thing to do,' she said.

Securing the grades to ensure entry to Scotland's top institutions, she chose to attend the University of Stirling: she had been advised that her chosen subject of Film and Media Studies would be best served there. The fact that the university also had a large sports department was an attraction for Hannah, and she went on to play for the university in both the British Universities Football competition and then at the European Universities Football competition in Spain. 'It was a very very good team,' she recalled. 'There was one person in my year that now plays for Scotland, Leanne Ross. And I remember playing against Gemma Faye, who is now Scotland's goalkeeper [...] so it was an amazing experience and great fun.'

Unlike Ross and Faye however, Hannah never sought to try and play for Scotland because she was determined to work in the media after university. During her studies she did work experience with the *Herald* and in Scottish television, and the latter gave her the chance to move straight into television after graduating: 'When I left university I got two jobs, one at the weekends editing football highlights for STV and one during the week working for GMTV, working on a children's TV programme called *Toonattik*.' Soon after working on *Toonattik*, Hannah moved to GMTV's Sunday political programme in London. Having loved documentaries as a child, the chance to move into more serious programming really appealed to her.

One Sunday in the run up to the 2007 Scottish election, Alex Salmond had been booked to come on the show as a guest. After the interview was over Hannah had the chance to speak with him: 'We just got chatting and then he said, "well why don't you think about coming to work for the SNP?"' She had been thinking about returning to Scotland and trying to secure a job as an on-screen reporter, but when the opportunity to work for the SNP came about she decided to go for it. She worked for the party in the run-up to the General Election and coordinated a lot of media as well as being responsible for the creation and launch of SNP TV, which was heavily used throughout 2007 and subsequent campaigns. After the victory for the party in the 2007 election, Hannah left the SNP headquarters to take on the role of setting up and managing Alex Salmond's new constituency office in Inverurie, where she remained for three years. Feeling that she needed a new challenge, Hannah moved to work for the American State Department at its consulate in Edinburgh, advising on Scottish issues. Her job at the American State Department was the perfect next step for her and it provided unusual challenges: 'We were once barricaded inside the consulate by a protest outside, and I had to escape out the back door and into the ambassador's car,' she laughingly recalled.

Initially she had intended to stay with the consulate for longer, but Hannah decided to move to Aberdeen to pursue a new career direction.

Having only really worked in the public sector or for public institutions, Hannah felt that she should gain experience of working in the private sector: 'I [found the] transition of moving into the Oil and Gas sector difficult in the beginning because I was completely out of my natural environment,' she said. However this new direction meant Hannah was able to test herself in a completely new setting while gaining valuable insight into an industry so vitally important to Scotland.

As the Referendum approached, Hannah felt that she wanted to get more involved in politics again. She initially spoke with Alex Salmond and felt ready to dive into the Yes campaign, but she was then headhunted by a company called Stork who offered her a role in supporting the setting-up of their business: 'It felt like too good an opportunity to pass up. So I worked across the UK, Africa, and Norway [...] and I felt I could still be involved with politics at arm's length and [be involved in the] campaign in the Referendum through Business for Scotland.' Yet the limited involvement Hannah was able to undertake was a constant source of frustration and the Referendum defeat convinced her that she couldn't stand on the sidelines any longer. She realised that if she was going to be involved in politics, she would have to go all in and stand for Parliament: 'I did have a wobble though,' she later admitted. 'I decided I was going to stand, and then decided against it, and it was Alex [Salmond] that talked me back into it.'

She left her position with Stork in December 2014 and put her name forward to stand in her home constituency of Livingston: 'Standing in your home constituency is a big deal. That chance to represent the place you grew up in really means something.' She won the selection for the SNP after running against Graeme Morrice. The election was always going to be tough for Hannah. She had to run in a constituency that, for many years, had been the heartland of the Scottish Labour Party – it was formally held by the Labour Foreign Secretary Robin Cook. However the result completely decimated the Labour vote, and Hannah received a 25.9% swing from the Labour Party. The night would be bittersweet for her however, as she saw Emma Harper lose out against David Mundell: 'I was really disappointed that Emma Harper didn't get elected. Throughout the election there was emails, and phone calls and we met up a few times [...] just to give each other moral support, so I was really disappointed for Emma.'

For Hannah, while the change in the Scottish political landscape shocked many, it was something she had long suspected: 'I think it had been coming for a long time, and people are so disengaged with the 'same old, same old' of politics. You can only give people second-class political representation for so long, and I think before that [...] we hadn't engaged people yet. When we did, and we gave them uniquely Scottish answers to uniquely Scottish questions, that started to resonate. And I think we've seen the response of that.'

49. GEORGE KEREVAN
EAST LOTHIAN

George Kerevan was born in Glasgow in 1949 at the tail end of the Attlee Labour Government. Raised in Drumchapel, George grew up in the heartlands of the Labour Party and witnessed the party's historic reforms take shape throughout the country: the mass building of council housing, the founding of the NHS, and the formation of the Welfare State.

George attended the University of Glasgow to undertake a Masters Degree in Politics Economy. While studying he also solidified his political beliefs, and after graduating with first-class honours he became heavily involved with the Labour Party, convinced by their advocacy of social justice and their commitment to delivering some form of home rule for Scotland. After university, he found his interests lay in academia and eventually George became a Lecturer of Economics with a specialism in energy policy. Alongside lecturing he pursued a writing career, writing for multiple newspapers and authoring multiple works on the past of, and future for, Scottish coal. He continued to lecture until 2000 when he was appointed as the Associate Editor of the *Scotsman*, a position he held until 2009.

Alongside his career in both academia and journalism, George was elected as a Labour councillor in Edinburgh in 1984. Having served as the city's chair of economic development, he is widely credited for helping to guide the economic revival of the city. During this time, he was also part of the team that founded and launched the Edinburgh Science Festival, and he also served on the board of both the Edinburgh International Festival and the Edinburgh Tourist Board, for which he was Chairman.

Despite being part of a left-wing council, following the election of Tony Blair as the Labour leader George became disillusioned with the national Labour Party. Their support for the Scottish Parliament sedated some of his concerns but as the party started to retreat over long-held positions on full employment and child benefits, he decided to officially defect to the SNP in 1996. However George didn't stand in an election for the SNP until 2010, when he came second to Labour's Sheila Gilmore in the Edinburgh East constituency.

During the 2014 Referendum, George became a major voice in the media by advocating for Scottish independence and for the economic credibility of an independent Scotland. He also wrote a book, *Scottish Independence: Yes or No*, alongside the *Daily Telegraph*'s Political Editor Alan Cochrane. After the Referendum George was selected as the SNP's candidate in East Lothian, although it was thought that the chances of winning the seat were slim, which George himself also acknowledged: the party had finished a distant fourth in the 2010 election, and with neither the city of Edinburgh nor the Lothian region having ever elected an SNP MP, the task seemed too much for a single election.

George nevertheless fought the seat and throughout the campaign he evoked the words and principles of a personal hero, East Lothian's former MP John P Mackintosh: 'He was very clear that home rule was something different from devolution,' he argued. 'Piecemeal devolution – granting a concession here and a concession there, a change here and a change there – has hardly resolved the issue of the Scottish desire for self-government.' George's campaign was also helped by and supported by Mackintosh's former Campaign Manager Arthur Greenan, which proved to be a point of personal pride for him.

Labour was also convinced that they would hold onto the East

Lothian seat: in the 2011 Scottish election in which the SNP defeated the Labour Party throughout Scotland, the East Lothian constituency had in fact re-elected a Labour MSP. East Lothian had also – like most of Edinburgh and the Lothians – heavily backed a No vote in the 2014 Referendum. Labour therefore hoped to bring about the same result as 2011, whereby a majority of No voters would back the Labour Party to ensure that the SNP were defeated.

As the election drew closer, national polling started to suggest that East Lothian was now likely to switch to the SNP. Indeed, the canvassing results that George received from his campaign team all pointed to the likelihood of an SNP victory. On election day George attended every polling station, seeking to understand the mood across the constituency: voter after voter told him that they planned to place their cross next to his name. The atmosphere was electric.

On election night the SNP secured a massive 20.1% swing from the Labour Party and wiped out a Labour majority of over 12,000. George secured a near 7,000 majority of his own, and although Labour disappeared off the map in Scotland that night, both he and his opponent exchanged kind remarks as they delivered their final speeches. Labour's exiting MP Fiona O'Donnell said: 'George Kerevan is a very lucky man to be representing such a great constituency.' He replied that he and the electorate of East Lothian had regarded Fiona as a 'first class constituency MP'.

'It has been hectic, exhilarating, and oft-times frustrating,' George said while reflecting on his short time at Westminster so far. In his maiden speech to the House of Commons George offered a glimpse into his imagined future of the United Kingdom: 'I think that within a generation we will have four independent parliaments in this Atlantic archipelago. We will co-operate, we will have a common market, we will discuss this and that, and we will probably have a common defence policy, but we will achieve that by recognising the right of the four nations – and certainly of Scotland – to be self-governing and independent. The family of nations can then treat each other as equals.'

50. OWEN THOMPSON
MIDLOTHIAN

Owen Thompson was elected as the MP for Midlothian in the 2015 General Election with a 50.6% share of the vote and a 30% swing. This is the first time the Midlothian constituency has had a non-Labour MP since the constituency's conception in 1955. Owen was raised in Loanhead after moving there from Glasgow at the age of seven, when his father became minister at Loanhead Parish Church. Owen attended Paradykes Primary School then Beeslack High School in Penicuik before he studied Accounting and Finance at Napier University.

Owen has been involved in the SNP from a very young age: he hadnded out leaflets with his uncle, brother, and father for various campaigns from the age of eight. After graduating from university Owen worked in the financial services industry before eventually turning his hand to local politics. He was first elected to the council in the Loanhead by-election in 2005 at the age of twenty-seven, becoming Scotland's youngest councillor at the time. He was then re-elected in the 2007 council election and again in the 2012 council election. He became leader of the council in November 2013, succeeding his party colleague Bob Constable.

In Owen's nine years in Midlothian Council he made significant improvements to his local area. He implemented park improvements in Roslin, Rosewell, and Loanhead; improved amenity space in Bilston; supported the groups developing the Kabin in Loanhead and the Auchendinny Centre, and more recently he has pushed for new primary schools at Paradykes in Loanhead and in Roslin.

While working for the council Owen was heavily involved in the Referendum campaign, which he described as 'madly busy' because 'I was out, not just on my own patch but around other bits of the country as well, working with various people and it was a hugely enjoyable experience doing the various public events: question and answer sessions and just engaging with so many new people. Obviously I was very disappointed by the result but the actual campaign and the experience itself was great. A big highlight for me was the volume of new people that were getting involved, turning out at the weekend to see the new faces of people who just wanted to be involved in politics. And for various, genuine reasons; there was no personal ambition, it was just because they wanted to do the best for their country.'

After the Referendum Owen said that he 'bounced back pretty quickly' because he was the leader of the council: 'If I was moping about then it would do absolutely nothing to help anyone else. I've been through so many elections, granted, not Referendums – elections that we've not done well in – I suppose that was a good training ground. Speaking to a few others who have been around elections for a long time I think that we are more able to get on and pick ourselves up again.'

The General Election campaign went by quickly: 'Oh, the campaign was a whirlwind. [Selection] to polling day was something like only 12 weeks, so it was a very short campaign. We managed to cover so much ground though, of course you were working with so many new activists and it was their first election so it was a good experience for them and their enthusiasm helped carry us all on. Also, we had been working so hard for two years in the Referendum then went straight into the campaign, and there was no break at all so there were a lot of folk getting quite tired by the end of it – but it was a great experience! The element of positivity left over from the Referendum campaign meant that people still wanted to be doing something and people were very keen to go. Now the General Election is done we've still got people going 'What do we do now?' very keen to get going with something else. It's great to see that engagement with politics.'

Owen discussed why he thought the 56 were elected: 'I think the election of the 56 is the people of Scotland very loudly saying that they rejected the Tory austerity agenda. The [issue of] independence is still very separate to a lot of people. We've still got a case to make and ultimately I think the Scottish people will tell us when they're ready for it. The welfare reforms have been particularly hard to stomach, especially when you think that – had Labour actually voted on it – there was a good chance we could have beaten the Tory party. That's massively frustrating. We just have to make sure we're representing our communities as best we can.'

Owen has varied interests outside of politics: 'Prior to election I was playing five-a-side [football] once a week. I've now joined the parliamentary football team, which is good fun. I've taken part in two games so far; one against the American Embassy and one against Cancer UK. The FA sponsor the team and the money all goes to charity so it's all very much for a good cause. Also, I've now done two Tough Mudders and I like to fundraise. I'm not the most traditionally fit-looking for that sort of thing and the ten-and-a-half-mile obstacle courses are good fun and for a good cause. Also, if I do have a spare moment, I am a bit of a sci-fi geek, so I enjoy catching up on films.'

Independence is still on the horizon for Owen: 'I still think I am going to see an independent Scotland [...] We'll see communities having a greater say and we'll see an abandonment of [the] market driven element that the Tories are pushing. We'll actually look out for each other and be far more considerate to each other and our communities.'

51. DEIDRE BROCK
EDINBURGH NORTH AND LEITH

The 56 has several members that are originally from outside of Scotland. Deidre Brock, however, definitely started life furthest afield: she was born in the Australian town of Albany in 1961. When Deidre was about eighteen months old her family moved to Perth in Western Australia. After going to school in Perth, Deidre enrolled at WAIT (Western Australian Institute of Technology) to study journalism, but she quickly realised that journalism was not for her and she swapped to a theatre arts course. After achieving a BA in English at WAIT, Deidre moved to the WA School of Arts where she studied a full-time drama course. In 1985 she moved to Sydney with her then-husband.

Deidre's interest in politics stems from her childhood: 'My dad and mum were always interested in politics and back home in Australia we always voted for the Labour party. I remember particularly when Gough Whitlan swept to power and the excitement of those times, which had an impression on me, and then also his dismissal by the governer general of Australia and all of the fallout from that. We used to discuss politics, my father was very interested in it. He had a lot of friends, funnily enough, most of whom were Liberal or Conservative voters because he always said what's the point of talking things over with people that agree with you all the time and he liked to sharpen his arguments on people who didn't. He worked at the Australian Broadcasting Corporation and he started off as a radio announcer in Albany and started working on TV doing a little bit of production and a little bit of directing. My father left the ABC at the time when there was another round of cutbacks from the government as the ABC was pretty much totally reliant on government funding. He and my mother opened a news agency and my father worked six-and-a-half days a week and had about two days off every year. At the same time, he presented a programme on films as a part-time thing. I had a lot of contact with people involved in politics and I'd often hear snatches of conversation at my parents' legendary parties.'

Deidre explained how her parents influenced her: 'My father and my mother shaped my politics and my attitude towards the world. My mother is a very kindly woman. Her mother was about ninety-two when she died and my mother used to go and visit some of her older friends after she died. These are the influences that shape you when you're growing up.' Deidre moved to Scotland in 1996 after visiting her sister in 1995: 'My sister was doing a round the world trip, came to Scotland, met a charming Scotsman and stopped and settled down. I came to Scotland a few weeks later and met my charming Scotsman and two children later, here I am. It was 1996 that I actually made the decision to move here to stay and then I had my first daughter in 1998 and my second in 2000.'

Deidre attributes her involvement in the SNP to her father-in-law: 'My father-in law has been in the party since he was seventeen and they have been part of the quiet group of workers who have quietly put up posters, stood outside polling stations, and shimmied up lamp-posts: all the hard work that got us to this point. I knew about the arguments for Scottish independence from [my parents-in-law] – my mother-in-law has been involved since her student days. [Their] persistence has been impressive as it's not always been an accepted thing to be in the party – I had a guy spit at me in the street once. My partner, as he puts it, grew up in the SNP putting out leaflets and he made me fully aware of the arguments. I think why wouldn't you want to run your own affairs? You all seem perfectly capable of doing it! We've had a taste of having Australia run from hundreds of miles away [...] and we've broken free of most of it and Australia has done quite well, thanks, so I don't see why we can't!'

While in Australia and then later in Scotland, Deidre worked a number of acting jobs including appearing in the soap opera *Home and Away*. In order to make ends meet around acting jobs Deidre worked as a PA; she then heard that one of the MSPs, Rob Gibson, was looking for a Parliamentary Assistant and she went forward for that. This was when Deidre became directly involved with the political world. Explaining her council career Deirdre said: 'After about three years working for Rob Gibson, I had some friends who convinced me that standing for council would be a good idea, so I did, and got in! I did that for eight years, starting as convener for culture and sport which was a steep learning curve. It was a new council, but given my background they thought I would have some knowledge of that, which I did. I then stood again, got in again and became depute Lord Provost. Over that time I discovered I liked helping people, it's a really satisfying thing to sort some problem that someone has had for a long time and you can come in and ask the right questions and point them in the right direction.'

Deidre was an integral part of the Referendum campaign in Leith and she attributes her decision to stand as an MP to the momentum of the campaign: 'We worked so hard on the run up to the Referendum and we were getting some very good results down here in Leith – you could see the mood shifting as the campaign wore on over the months. There was so much excitement and interest from people who were never involved in politics. We were then quite shocked by the 60/40 No/Yes result, but we didn't know what the proportions were before so it must have shifted quite considerably. After that I just felt like I wanted to feel like I was still in the momentum and be a part of something that I knew would be an historic election. I wanted to take the skills I had acquired from the previous eight years in politics and bring them forward. I'm really so chuffed that I've been elected to represent this area because it is a fantastic constituency and there's so much going on for it.'

Deidre's interests outside of politics reflect her background in the arts and her enthusiasm for Scottish culture: 'I love reading [...] I spend so much time reading reports and background material [so] reading for pleasure is a treat and I love films [...] I also love history and visiting museums – I'm always the one who walks through and everyone is ahead of me and I'm behind reading the label on every item. I love reading about the history of the UK and Scotland. I also love drawing, sewing, tapestry, and my garden. I love traditional music and attending ceilidhs. I'm passionate about the Gaelic language and culture; I learnt it for years and my children went to Gaelic school at Tollcross. I played my part with the council getting the Gaelic school in Bonnington [and] I try to promote Gaelic as much as possible as it's a beautiful language and culture and I think Scotland would be much the poorer for not having it, especially as so many of the symbols of what the world sees as Scottish comes from that background.'

Although she is inspired by Scotland's cultural history, Deidre's eye is to the future: 'I think another independence Referendum is inevitable. When I don't know, but it will almost certainly hinge on something dramatic happening like Scotland being pulled out of the EU against its wishes. I just cannot see why this country can't do a better job of running itself than by a parliament hundreds of miles away with none of its focuses on the country. I see so many examples of small successful European countries without oil, but with people with grit and determination like Scotland. I think the SNP government has shown the way, even with limited powers at its command in running the country. I believe utterly in the strengths and abilities of the Scottish people.'

52. JOANNA CHERRY QC
EDINBURGH SOUTH WEST

Joanna Cherry QC is the SNP Justice and Home Affairs Spokesperson in the House of Commons and she has a wealth of experience outside of the political sphere. Born and brought up in Edinburgh, Joanna 'went to Holy Cross Primary which is down near New Haven in Trinity, and then for secondary school, I went to a small independent girls' school called St. Margaret's Convent which used to be in Whitehouse Loan in Edinburgh but isn't there any longer – it shut down in the 80s. I enjoyed school – Holy Cross was a big Catholic Primary with a very diverse mix of pupils and some really great teachers. The Convent was a much smaller school but, again, there were some really influential teachers with whom I've kept in touch, including my Latin and French teacher who's been a huge support to me during the election campaign.'

'When I was a teenager I wanted to be a Labour MP! After that ambition, I thought I wanted to be a journalist but I had a very good English teacher who talked me into doing Law which was very good advice; I think it was the best career choice for me at the time. So, I thought about Oxford and Cambridge, but I decided I wanted to stay in Scotland to practise law so I applied to various Scottish universities and decided on Edinburgh at the end.' At Edinburgh University Joanna gained a first class Bachelor of Law honours degree in 1988, a Master of Law degree in 1989, then a Diploma in Legal Practice in 1990.

Joanna had a very successful career in law, moving from being a solicitor to an advocate to Standing Junior Counsel to the Scottish Government from 2003 to 2008. She was then an Advocate Depute and Senior Advocate Depute from 2008 until 2011, while in 2009 she was appointed to the lofty rank of Queen's Counsel. Joanna's journey into the SNP happened in parallel to her successful career: 'Well, when I was at university I was very involved with Labour Students as well as CND and I remained a member of the Labour party after university – in fact, one of my contemporaries was Douglas Alexander. I was, however, always in favour of home rule – my father, as a nationalist, was very influential. I suppose I was always in favour of independence but it didn't really seem that big an issue in the Thatcher years – the main issue seemed to be to fight Thatcherism. I was also very involved in the campaign for Scottish Assembly.'

'I became disillusioned with the Labour Party because I felt that their heart wasn't in home rule, and I still believe that. I think there are many decent individuals in Labour, Dennis Canavan comes to mind, but I think [that] many people just saw home rule as a sort of bourgeois distraction and I felt, within the Labour party, that I was very unpopular because I was so in favour of home rule and campaigning for the Scottish Assembly. I became disillusioned with them over that and I also became disillusioned over poll tax, which was really the final straw for me, as Labour had fifty Scottish MPs but seemed unable to really take any meaningful, principled stance against it in a way that would actually protect people from what was really an iniquitous tax. So I left the Labour party and started voting SNP in the mid-90s before joining the party in 2008.'

Joanna was very active in the Scottish Referendum campaign: 'The year I got involved in the Referendum was one of the happiest years of my life. For many years I wasn't terribly politically active because I held public offices, which meant I couldn't be. Initially I got involved in a little bit of local campaigning with my local Yes group but then a colleague and I set up Lawyers for Yes, for which I ended up really becoming the public face and leading. It was immensely rewarding.

I met many interesting people from other sectorial groups in the Yes movement and indeed some very interesting people on the No side who I've kept in touch with. It was just so exciting to get involved in such a well-informed debate and see that there were so many ordinary people who were not normally involved in politics so engaged in it and reading stimulating stuff, like Lesley Riddoch's book *Blossom* and Andy Wightman's book about land reform. I'm not saying I agree with everything they say, but I think their ideas were immensely stimulating. Somebody said that Scotland had awoken from a long sleepwalk and I think that was true, and I was privileged to have participated in that, to have been alive through that and then, after the Referendum, there was a brief period of depression and then everything seemed to pick up again and I got really involved in the SNP selection process.'

Talking about differences between the political sentiments of Scottish and English voters, Joanna believes that the Referendum ignited a political awareness in people that the English and Welsh don't necessarily have: 'I think that Scotland is more left leaning and liberal in its sentiments. I know people would dispute that but I think anyone who came [...] down here and looked at the way debate is conducted in Westminster, compared to the Scottish Parliament, couldn't really seriously refute that. I also think [that] anyone who voted No who spent a significant time down here might be persuaded to be a Yes voter.'

Outside of politics and law Joanna is passionate about travelling: 'Just under ten years ago, around about the time of my fortieth birthday, I took some time out of my career and I spent six months travelling around Australia and New Zealand which was immense [...] I was very lucky [to have had] financial independence, [meaning] I was able to do that at the time. It was very rewarding; I think that travel really broadens the mind. I also like reading. I used to like exercising like swimming and walking but you get a lot of exercise walking around Westminster. It's a long walk from my office to the chamber!'

Joanna's greatest influence is Alex Salmond: 'He has been such an inspirational leader. He achieved what I thought ten years ago was unachievable which is an SNP government: a minority government, and then a majority government. He created the conditions for the Referendum and he has had to put up with so much abuse and so much unfair criticism. I also really admire him because he is unselfish and he sacrificed himself by resigning the day after the Referendum – a lot of people wouldn't have done that – because he knew it would create the conditions for us to capitalise on what was to come. Now he's down here it really benefits the group to have such an experienced UK parliamentarian here so that's the person I most admire in my political life – by a mile actually.'

As a QC, Joanna was well prepared for the tradition and ceremony of Parliament and she isn't as frustrated by it to the same extent as some of the other members of the 56. There are, however, aspects of Westminster's system that particularly irk her: 'I find it very frustrating, as a lawyer, that ministers do not answer the question. The Prime Minister so often at Prime Minister's Question Time really doesn't answer a single question and another good example is David Mundell at Scottish Questions – his evasion was totally outrageous. I feel that the Speaker ought to intervene, a bit like a judge, and tell the ministers to answer the question. I do also find the baying and shouting during the questions very inappropriate, although I noticed they toned it down a bit recently which I suspect is because of the adverse public reaction to what happened in the chamber the first week after the elections.'

Although she hopes to address many issues, Joanna's key aim in Parliament 'is to prevent repeal of the Human Rights Act and to make sure that the United Kingdom remains a member of the European Court of Human Rights. Also, to make sure that the Tory party's prejudice against the Human Rights Act and the ECHR doesn't impact on the important place of human rights in the devolved settlement.' She also has a clear vision for a future Scotland: 'an independent Scottish republic with a written constitution, protection of minority rights, constitutional court. I think I'd like to see us model ourselves on the modern South African constitution and their constitutional court: a wonderful constitution that encompasses social and economic rights as well as basic human rights. Also, I would like Scotland to be a constitutional democracy with a president rather that a monarch.'

53. MICHELLE THOMSON
EDINBURGH WEST

On several occasions Michelle Thomson has described herself as someone who was 'always politically aware, but never politically active' before the Referendum campaign. Since then, she has made up for lost time by speaking at over ninety events during the Referendum and running a very successful General Election campaign which saw her elected into the seat of Edinburgh West which had been held by the Liberal Democrats over the previous three elections.

Michelle grew up in Bearsden, where she attended both primary and secondary school. Early on Michelle sought to question and challenge the status quo as she explained: 'In primary six I put up my hand during a lesson on the Queen and said, "I'm not sure why the Queen has so many houses when other people don't even have one". For my trouble I got taken to the front of the class and given the belt. The same teacher [that] same year was also talking about God and I put up my hand and said, "How do you know there is a God and how do you know that your God is the right one?" I'd been reading this book and I knew there were lots of gods and lots of religions. Rather than saying 'this is quite unusual from a ten-year old', I got taken out to the front of the class and belted. It was that point I decided that, although I was contracting to society to learn information, I was not contracting to society to learn how to think or what to think. That probably framed how I wanted to live my life and ultimately led me to where I am today, because I like to challenge things.'

After school Michelle went on to study music and specialised in piano at the Royal Scottish Academy of Music and Drama. Although Michelle's life could have taken a vastly different path, confidence in her musical talent led to her audition for the RSAMD: 'I auditioned in secret because my father, who is an engineer [...] got me a job interview as a trainee clerkess [which] was a fate worse than death. He said I should just go and get a wee secure job, which he was obviously thinking because I was a girl and I had two elder brothers. I went to the wee job interview and the guy was asking about me and said, "What would you choose if we offer this job but you get into the Academy?" and I replied saying it was a total no brainer – of course I would go there! He said to my father, "I would love to offer her a job but she quite clearly wants to do more." My dad was angry with me for turning down something, and I was angry with him because I wondered whether that was the height of his ambition for me as his daughter. I think we now both conclude that I made the right decision, but not at the time. All of us come to a point in our life where we say 'I'm not going to accept other people's limitations of me' and that has correlated with many people in Scotland who should push back and say they have more ambition.'

When asked how she made the jump from working as a professional musician to working in financial services, Michelle laughed and replied: 'the first is because I like putting myself in somewhere I have no experience. The other reason was that I met my husband, who was an opera singer, and a very gifted musician. I knew quickly [that] we were serious, but he didn't look ahead like I did in terms of planning for the future, he lived in the moment. He was doing major roles in opera companies, big, solo roles, and he'd earn a lot in a night but wouldn't know when he'd be working again. That made it hard to plan financially. The third reason is because I had ended up as a musical director in a theatre and I had used IT equipment to write music. This was in the early days, and at the time it was truly revolutionary using a synthesizer and a sampler to create music. I thought that IT was so pervasive. I became really interested and went off to do a Masters in IT.'

'I bet my brother a fiver that I could get a job as a programmer. He was an actuary and is very bright, and at that time in the manner of sibling rivalry he thought that musicians are just flakes, like 'Oh, darling I can feel a symphony coming on.' I won the bet! I quite quickly realised that I wasn't very good at computer programming but I found that I was quite good at planning and organising, so I went into project management [...] delivering IT changes and large scale business changes. It was all about good communication. That was all when my children were young and growing up so these jobs worked very well at that time in my life.'

Alex Salmond was always a very influential figure to Michelle. Drawing on an example from when she worked at Standard Life, she explained: 'everyone else [in the senior management team] picked one of the executives at Standard Life [as someone who inspired them] which I thought was very lame. I picked Alex Salmond and that created some surprise. From a leadership perspective he is the person that thinks differently and frames out a different way. Even though some people love him and some people hate him, he has made it his life's work to try and take Scotland forward. He is a very clever man. He could have made a fortune in the city but instead he chose to do this. He has genuinely inspired me as he said, "this is what I believe to be true" in a time when it was very unpopular.'

In 2009 Michelle moved away from financial services and set up her own property business. Despite the financial crisis, her business was successful and she remembers telling someone when she first started 'No global financial crisis is going to get in my way!' With so much experience in business and having started her own small company, when the Referendum came about in 2014 Michelle was asked to go on the board of the fledgling Business for Scotland and she soon realised she wanted to fully commit to the cause: 'I wanted to do the whole thing full-time, the whole way. By that point I had a great deal of life experience, a good level of financial services experience, a good level of business experience, and I knew how to meet and communicate with people. I wanted to look at the business case for independence

– not just looking at the risks but the opportunities, which I felt were considerable. Let's also give voice to small businesses as I was fed up hearing the voice of huge businesses, multinationals, headquartered in London that had no relevance to us whatsoever. Also, a big theme for me has always been ambition. I don't want to be told what we can't do, I want to foster a feeling of positivity and drive in people at every level! I literally spent most of my time doing media as they needed a business voice, but to be honest I think they liked having a female business voice. I liked doing it, and I suspect that's probably from the drama side in my past, learning how to come across. I did a lot of media, I think I must have spoken all over Scotland.'

Michelle decided to run for parliament because of her experiences over the Referendum campaign: 'I decided late on in the Referendum that if it was a No I had to keep on going because I had made a promise to myself to use all of my energy and all of my drive to try and get a Yes vote. I was relentless. I felt that I had to keep going fostering change like I had been, so it was an easy decision. I remember my husband saying, "You are having a laugh!" when I said I was going to go to an election campaign. I just felt that it's really important to give a voice for people like me. I want to see a level of social justice in Scotland and I understand economically how a strong economy can support the public services you want and I want to see more of an accent on supporting small business and innovation which will drive us forward. I felt that I have a fairly unique perspective which would add to the team.'

Michelle has a set of clear views and one of the things that is most important to her is debate: 'People have always described me as a bit different, and that's not different in inverted commas meaning socially unacceptable! In some respects that's why I am attracted by politics – if someone says black is black is black I will always say white and likewise the other way around. I don't necessarily always argue against things in public, especially now I'm a politician, but I always ask: why do you want me to think that? I like being contrary, and it's healthy to always think of the alternative.'

Michelle Thomson MP resigned the SNP party whip on 29 September 2015 and was suspended from the party, pending the outcome of an investigation.

54. TOMMY SHEPPARD
EDINBURGH EAST

Tommy Sheppard is a familiar name in the world of politics. Having been involved in the Labour Party extensively from the 80s through to 1997 when he held several positions of authority including Assistant General Secretary under John Smith in 1994, he left the party officially in 2003. In 2012 Tommy became the Edinburgh South Organiser of the Yes Scotland campaign and joined the SNP officially in 2014. In the General Election this year Tommy won the constituency of Edinburgh East with 49.2% of the vote.

Tommy was born in 1959 in Coleraine, County Londonderry, which he describes as 'a sort of protestant garrison town'. At the age of six Tommy's father got a payout from an industrial injury: this enabled him to attain a mortgage on a little house in Portstewart. Tommy attended Portstewart primary school and then went on to Coleraine Academical Institution, his local grammar school. Tommy left Ireland in 1977 to go to Aberdeen University to study Medicine, but he graduated with a degree in Politics and Sociology in 1982. He was elected Vice President of the National Union of Students that same year, and moved to London.

Tommy first became aware of, and interested in, politics around the age of fourteen. Talking about this initial interest he said: 'it was actually environmental politics that I got into – the big campaign in the 1970s was about the Windscale nuclear reprocessing plant, and it threw up a big debate about the future of nuclear power and I got heavily involved in that. At that time I joined Friends of the Earth and other groups back then – long before it was trendy! That was my way in as it were, and then when you get involved in one issue you develop a perspective in new places in the context of other issues, and you begin to form a worldview. I went through an explosion of ideas between about sixteen and eighteen. I was like a sponge soaking up various radical left-wing ideas and trying to compute them. They all settled down by the time I was about twenty into a left democratic perspective on life and that's pretty much where I am now – I haven't changed!'

Tommy then went on to describe his journey towards joining the SNP: 'I joined the Labour Party when I was around twenty, in 1979. I think it was just before Margaret Thatcher got elected for the first time. I had been active in the devolution vote back in 1979 and campaigned for and voted for devolution when I was in Aberdeen. Looking back, it was a different kettle of fish from the 1997 Referendum and the Referendum last year: it didn't really seem to catch fire the way either of those did. I joined the Labour Party and I was [in it] for about twenty years. I got reasonably far up the greasy pole, became number two in the Scottish party to Jack McConnell, and was appointed under John Smith and asked to leave under Tony Blair. The Labour Party sort of left me at the end of the 1990s when Blair got into his stride and I think I left when he invaded Iraq – that wasn't the reason, it was almost coincidental as I was leaving anyway – but it takes time to get around to cancelling a direct debit doesn't it? I haven't been active in the Labour Party since about 1999, I think that was the last meeting I attended. Really, for me, the final straw was when they kept me off the panel of candidates for the Scottish Parliament – that's when it signalled to me that the Labour Party didn't see any future with me in it. It began a process of disillusionment that saw me step back from having been very politically active to still being politically interested but not active in anything. I was on the board of a few organisations like Scottish Left Review and other things so I kept my hand in, but I really concentrated during the noughties on building up my business, The Stand Comedy Club, and taking it from what started as a hobby into a business employing over fifty people.'

'The reason why I'm in the SNP is because I became convinced during the noughties of the case for independence and that independence was a way of achieving the type of democratic social reforms that I'd always believed in and still believe in. Put simply, it would be easier to make these changes in a small northern European country of five and a half million people, where the majority of the population were quite relaxed about them, rather than continue to be part of a much larger country where there was a majority hostile to that kind of change.'

Tommy was very involved in the Referendum campaign in Edinburgh and explained that after the result he was 'gutted, like everyone. I was in a sort of fugue state for the weekend after it. I felt it was so near, but yet so far, and I was so disappointed. But after that weekend I began to appreciate that we had, from a standing start, run a campaign to take Scotland out of the fifth most powerful country on the face of the planet, taking on the entire state apparatus, the entire establishment, the forces of conservativism and big business. What's apparent now, which we only began to see as the mist lifted, was the process of getting voted [...] certainly for those who came down to support the Yes side, [the process] was liberating, inspiring, educational. It was creative and it's not something you could just put back in the bottle. It's something that happened and it's not going to un-happen. Like so many other people, I took the view in the week after the Referendum that the next phase [...] was to engage politically and parliamentarily to advance the cause for change and the means to do it is with the SNP, which is why I joined the SNP. I'm not from a traditional nationalist background at all – I've said before I don't really describe myself as a nationalist. I don't think the SNP can be simply dismissed as a nationalist party – the potency of the SNP now is that it has combined a sort of civic nationalism and pride in one's country with a social democratic program that the Labour party have abandoned and those two things together make two very good bedfellows.'

Since becoming an MP, Tommy has been particularly displeased with Westminster's traditions and conventions: 'it's appalling, it's like a pantomime. You can look around and see the history of the architecture and it can be easy to get seduced, so you have to keep reminding yourself why you're here. It's not to look at the works in a museum, which is what this place is. We're not here to make gesture politics and stick our arses up to the speaker. I was told off yesterday for addressing someone in the second person plural, you're never supposed to do that apparently, you have to refer to them in the third person all the time! But we'll get on top of these little foibles of the standing orders and use and exploit them to advance what people sent us here for. We're here to engage with this place, we're here to push it to the limits [...], we're not just here just as observers.'

When asked who he sees as major influences on his life Tommy said: 'I sometimes feel I'm so un-reverential that I appear inhuman, you know? There were some figures in the Labour left when I was younger who were inspirational like Tony Benn when he was on form. Margo [MacDonald] was inspirational and I knew her in her latter years and it was a privilege to do so. She was the ultimate icon. There are people who have influenced me and who I have tremendous respect for but I don't really have anyone on a pedestal.'

Looking forward for Scotland, Tommy wants a just society with republican values: 'I'd like to see an independent Scotland where a left social democratic consensus is the settled will of the people, where it's taken for granted that we live in a society where people help each other, and [where] we measure the quality of the society by how it treats the weakest and the most vulnerable. Also to have a country where we look outwards to the world, to Europe and to the rest of Britain as well and provide inspirational solidarity where we can, but most importantly where we use the wealth and resources of our country for the benefit of all our people. That's what I'd like to see and maybe [this won't happen] in my lifetime but [...] I would like to see a fully democratic Scotland which means that it should be a republic where the people, according to law, elect their leader, and patronage and feudalism are put to rest forever.'

55. RICHARD ARKLESS
DUMFRIES AND GALLOWAY

Richard Arkless defeated Labour's Russell Brown with 41.4% of the vote, taking the seat from the MP who has held it since its creation in 2005. Richard was born in Stranraer in 1975 – where he lives now – but he lived in East London until the age of eight. He initially went to St Francis of Assisi School just behind Maryland Point in Forest Gate and the family resided in Earlham Grove, within five miles of Westminster. After a stint in London, his parents moved back Stranraer and Richard attended Stranraer Academy.

Richard went to university twice: firstly in 1994 to undertake a BA in Financial Services and Risk Management at Glasgow Caledonian University, and secondly, to study law at Strathclyde University between 2004 and 2006. Speaking of university he said: '[Glasgow Caledonian] had just converted from a polytechnic to a university so there was a real working-class feel to it at the time. I've no idea what it's like now but it's almost unrecognisable from what it was back then, but I had some great times there and thoroughly enjoyed my time there.'

Like many of the 56, Richard's political interest started young but his actual involvement was sparked by the Referendum: 'I was always interested in politics. I was always fairly opinionated and I was the guy at the front of the Modern Studies class who was constantly giving the teacher a hard time by putting my hand up all the time because I had a whole range of incoherent views and beliefs and opinions at that point which have now been redefined and refined over the years.' Richard then explained how his involvement in the SNP stemmed from his interest in economics: 'I've always been a floating voter, and it may be a surprise to some people to know that despite being an SNP MP that back in the late 90s I voted No for devolution. I didn't think it was a good idea at the time and I was wrong, but I've come full circle to where I am at the moment in terms of political beliefs.'

'Independence was something that I didn't support at the time but when they [the SNP] did get elected to lead the Scottish Government I felt a constitutional obligation to start looking into it and I felt that they were obviously a serious party with serious views. It was then that my mind got re-engaged in politics and I started to reconsider the question of independence [...] in detail over three or four years. Around the time, just before the majority government were elected in 2011, I found my resting place in terms of my ideology in the constitution, and found I was a full supporter of Scottish independence.'

'[Researching] in those three or four years was [...] trying to find the right answers to the preconceptions that I had in my mind that needed to be dismantled. One of the other catalysts, in 2007, coincided with me qualifying as a fully-fledged lawyer and at law school they teach you to go to the source document – you don't rely on hearsay – you have to go and find the answer for yourself.'

Before becoming an MP, a concern for Richard was the economics of Europe: 'I remember being a kid on holiday with my mum and dad at a time when the Tory Government, I think it was Nigel Lawson [as Chancellor], had to increase interest rates by 10% in one day as part of the exchange rate mechanism crisis that we were going through at the time.' Richard explained how economics remains a key issue that he wants to address as an MP: 'I would describe myself as a social democrat in that I passionately believe in social justice. That's not to say that we're totally different from the rest of the UK but for me it's the interaction between social justice and a growing economy that makes a true social democrat and coming from an economic background that was always my interest. It was the economics that first lit my flame and then as I started to understand what you could do in politics in terms of creating a fairer society and that you didn't need to have this literal black and white centre-right economic view and that you could combine the two – you could combine an incentive-based structure and you could combine an economy but you could manage the outcomes better and create a much more just society. As the Scottish Government has brought forward things like the homeless act where homelessness is essentially illegal in Scotland, the egalitarian policies like free tuition fees really resonated with me and it became apparent that a true social democrat could fight the corner of both a growing economy and a just society. It's the link between those two that really fires me up outside of the constitution.'

Richard then spoke about his experience of the Referendum campaign: 'I campaigned incredibly hard during the Referendum for almost a year, I worked for an organisation called Business for Scotland, and I spoke at over forty public meetings mostly across the south of Scotland and I put my heart and soul into it and so did my wife. We shelved our business and our lives for the final months of the campaign so we'd invested not only time but a great deal of emotional energy. [...] I was driving to the count and I heard the exit poll at five past ten [and] until that point I was 100% sure that we were going to win it. It was a very quick comedown from five past ten until the early hours when it became apparent that we weren't going to win and it was devastation. But bubbling in the back of my mind was the flame within myself that I'd ignited and [...] as soon as David Cameron stepped out of Downing Street the morning after the Referendum and tied the entire process into English Votes for English Laws, I turned around to my wife and said, "It's game on again. And you know what I'm going to say, don't you?" She said, "What, Richard?" I said, "We're going to dedicate our entire life to this cause", and she agreed and from that moment on we had something to look forward to. It's easy for me because I've been convinced of this question for five or six years, whereas some of my colleagues in team 56 have been fighting their entire adult life for this cause.'

When asked who particularly inspires him in life, Richard replied:

'My dad always told me never to have heroes so if I were to be completely honest with you it would be two or three football players that I've known all my time. In terms of politics, one figure I revere a lot is Nelson Mandela. I was politically engaged when he came out of prison and we studied him in the apartheid classes in Modern Studies and it was something that gripped me a lot at the time. I've always been inspired by my parents, my wife inspires me, and recently in terms of this process I owe a lot of thanks and credit to the MSPs in my particular region who have given me confidence: Aileen Mcleod and Jody McAlpine.'

Outside of the political sphere, Richard also expressed his love of sport and his family: 'My passion at the moment is my family. That's [been] my passion since I got married, and everything I do, directly or indirectly, I'm doing for them, whether it's for my kids for a better future or for my wife to give her the life that she deserves. I've always been a big sporting fan. I was a poor eleven handicapper back in the day when I had time to play golf. These days I prefer watching rugby to football but I did hold a season ticket to one for the Glasgow teams for seventeen years – the green and white side of the divide. I've always had a natural inclination to support Celtic and I went to the world cup in 1990 as a fifteen year old, and I literally dream from time to time of going back to a world cup with a tartan army. I'd love to see, beyond anything, either a Scotland rugby team or a Scotland football team just get to the second round.'

56. CALUM KERR
BERWICKSHIRE, ROXBURGH AND SELKIRK

Calum Kerr was born in Galashiels and grew up in the Scottish Borders, regularly moving around to accommodate his father's employment as a teacher. His family eventually settled in the town of Peebles, where his dad secured a permanent post at the local school, while his mum, a trained nursery nurse, was also able to find work. Having been raised in the rural areas of the Scottish Borders, Calum loved the community spirit of small towns. Growing up with a close group of friends, the opportunity to explore the world around him every day made his childhood fantastic. When it came to deciding where to go to university, Calum was adamant he didn't want to go to a large city: 'I had always lived in smaller towns, so St Andrews was a happy medium.'

After originally being accepted to study a degree in History and Management, Calum quickly discovered that the management side of his degree did not interest him. Eventually, he dropped Management in favour of History. After graduating, he had no plan of action for what he wanted to do next, so he moved back home to live with his parents in Peebles. Calum got a job in the local job centre and used the time to try to figure out where his future lay.

Calum's dad had encouraged him to consider applying to be a

teacher, but his application was turned down: 'They rightly spotted that I didn't actually want to be a teacher,' he reflected. An unfortunate accident while playing rugby convinced him he needed to find a real job, so Calum travelled to London for an assessment day with an advertising and marketing agency: 'On the day, a guy from Philips Communications offered me a job. For a graduate that had been lazing around for ten months to get offered a job with a car and a decent amount of money was a bit of a shock. So I bit his hand off.'

On accepting the post at Philips Communications, Calum moved down to Cambridge before moving to London and joining Nortel. It wasn't long before Calum had to transfer back up to Scotland and settle back into life in Peebles, as he explained: 'I was out with my boss one night and she asked me where I saw my career going. And I just said that I wasn't someone who thought they had to be the Managing Director in five years etc. I was just interested in doing a good job and getting the chance to move back up to Scotland, then within a week she came back to me with an opportunity in Scotland.'

It was in 2009, however, after the company he was working for went into administration and faced possible bankruptcy, that he started to revaluate his life and the choices he had made: 'It was brutal, but it did wake me up. I started to think 'what are my priorities in life and what I'm I going to do to make a difference?" From that moment, his life changed from being career-focused to much more community-centred: he became the treasurer of Peebles Highland Games and started to coach his eldest son's football team as well as joining the SNP. By now part of the SNP, Calum was determined to get stuck into the Referendum campaign. The first meeting about the Referendum hosted by Yes Scotland in Galashiels did however turn out to be very frustrating for Calum: he attended the meeting hoping to find a plan of action but instead he left without any real idea of what was to happen next. At the next meeting he decided to take a bit more control, and by the end of it the group had set up Yes Tweeddale.

Over the course of the next two years Calum worked around the Scottish borders trying to set up local Yes groups in communities and then bring them together via an umbrella body called Yes Scottish Borders, as he explained: 'I became the lead volunteer, and it totally took over my life. I told my work that there would be evenings and weekends that they would just not be able to reach me because this [was] really important to me.' It all led to the most devastating night of his life, when Scotland voted No. The devastation was compounded when the Scottish Borders voted at a two-to-one ratio against independence. Calum commented: 'The day after the Referendum I was an emotional wreck. Lots of people were texting me saying how proud they were, and on came the tears. I had a day of that and then I said we are not giving up.'

Although the Referendum result was awful for Calum, through the actual campaign he had discovered a passion within himself that he hadn't known before: 'I realised that I wanted to do this, going back to my work just wouldn't be the same thing. At that point I wasn't saying I was going to run [in the General Election], but my wife was the one that said to me that if I wanted to pursue it then I should. Once she said that, that was it. I must have told everyone in five minutes so she couldn't go back on it.'

Calum was selected for his home constituency of Berwickshire, Roxburgh, and Selkirk, and from the outset it was the most unlikely constituency to elect an SNP MP in the whole of Scotland. Because of this, Calum didn't start off thinking that he could win the seat; rather, his aim was to come a strong second to the Conservatives to show that it was the SNP that was now their opposition, not the Liberal Democrats. However, Nicola Sturgeon's performance and the canvass results started to give him hope that victory was not impossible.

The Ashcroft Poll was a key moment of the campaign for Calum because it put the SNP ahead of the Liberal Democrats and it was evident to everyone that the seat would either go to him or to the Tories: 'I always believed there was an anti-Tory majority in the seat,' he said. The campaign had focused on Calum's ability to mobilise that group, but when the exit polls came out on election night, Calum was torn between being happy at the idea of 56 SNP MPs and devastated at the likelihood of another Conservative government. He did however have an immense pride in the SNP campaign: 'I felt we had run an amazing campaign that we were proud of and whatever happened we were going to run the Tories close.'

As the night progressed the campaign team started to feel more confident. Although they were down by a few thousand votes, the large towns hadn't yet been counted and it was predicted that a lot of SNP support would come from these areas. By 4am the official count had the SNP winning by more than 300 votes, and while the Tories called for a recount, at this point Calum knew he had won the constituency.

In his maiden speech to the House of Commons, Calum reaffirmed the principles that had helped him become the first non-Liberal Democrat MP for his constituency since 1955: 'We have not come to this place to agitate for independence. We are here to protect and promote Scotland's interests, and to stand with all those who will oppose austerity and work for freedom, human rights, and social justice. We want to be constructive, and to fulfil our constitutional role in opposing this Tory Government – and, at times, opposing the official Opposition too. Our 56-strong SNP team were elected to this place in the most powerful affirmation of a peoples' democratic will ever seen within the Union. The move towards a better, fairer, more democratic Scotland took a huge leap forward in May. This is our time. We come from an ancient nation, but we bring new thinking.'

JOSH BIRCHAM

Josh Bircham was born in Edinburgh and grew up in the small village of St Madoes, outside Perth. After finishing school, he moved on to study English at the University of Aberdeen. There, he was both the co-head editor and the head of production for the student newspaper, The Gaudie. He currently lives in Edinburgh where he works in communications.

GRANT COSTELLO

Grant was born in Bellshill, on the 23rd of December 1992. He grew up in East Kilbride, before moving to study Politics and International Relations at the University of Aberdeen. While at university served as Chairman of the Scottish Youth Parliament and co-edited the university student newspaper, The Gaudie, with Josh. After graduating university he was hired as the SNP's Westminster Social Media Press Officer.